Civil Disobedience and Beyond

Civil Disobedience and Beyond

Law, Resistance and Religion in South Africa

CHARLES VILLA-VICENCO

DAVID PHILIP · CAPE TOWN
WM. B. EERDMANS · GRAND RAPIDS

First published in 1990 in southern Africa by David Philip Publishers (Pty) Ltd, 208 Werdmuller Centre, Claremont 7700, South Africa.

Published in 1990 in the United States of America by Wm. B. Eerdmans Publishing Co., 255 Jefferson Ave., SE, Grand Rapids, Michigan 49503

Printed in South Africa

ISBN 0-86486-144-3 (David Philip)
ISBN 0-8028-0526-4 (Wm. B. Eerdmans)

LIBRARY OF CONGRESS CATALOGING-IN-PUBLICATION DATA

Villa-Vicencio, Charles
    Civil disobedience and beyond : law, resistance and religion in South Africa / Charles Villa-Vicencio.
        p.   cm.
    Includes bibliographical references.
    ISBN 0-8028-0526-4
    1. Government, Resistance to--Religious aspects--Christianity.
2. Government, Resistance to--South Africa. 3. Revolutions-
-Religious aspects--Christianity. 4. South Africa--Politics and government--1970- 6. South Africa--Church history--20th century.
I. Title.
BV630.2.V54   1990
241'.621'0868--dc20   90-30862
                                                       CIP

Printed by Clyson Printers (Pty) Ltd, Maitland, Cape, South Africa

Contents

Preface

After the manuscript of this book was submitted to the publisher, the Mass Democratic Movement (MDM), an alliance of anti-apartheid organisations formed around the United Democratic Front (UDF) and the Congress of South African Trade Unions (COSATU), launched the 1989 defiance campaign. It came as a vivid reminder of the historic defiance campaign of 1952.

Since the launch of the 1989 defiance campaign the character of the liberation struggle in South Africa has changed dramatically, giving further credence to the suggestion that the struggle has entered a new phase. The history of more than three hundred years of struggle which forms the historical context within which the theological themes are discussed in this book has been taken a further step forward. The theological lessons learned within this history have again been underlined – *Christians are required in resistance and defiance to join others in struggling against oppression.*

During the months of the defiance campaign evidence has also emerged of further disintegration of the apartheid state. In the Transkei, for example, there is every indication of the Bantustan system rebounding against the very system that gave it birth. Bantu Holomisa, the military ruler of the Transkei, has insisted that it is the right of Transkeians to decide whether to return to a united South Africa after apartheid is replaced with majority rule. The presence of death squads linked to the South African Police, with the responsibility to kill opponents of the state, is now being openly alleged and debated. As this Preface is written it has been announced that actual arrests have been made following the assassination of political activists David Webster and Anton Lubowski earlier in the year. Some police officers have openly rebelled against the police brutality and the sense of confidence with which the present regime formerly executed its repression is no longer as obvious as it once was.

Government leaders are stating that apartheid is to be removed, suggesting a policy crisis bigger than anything this regime has ever faced. When an oppressive regime no longer believes its own ideology it is a sign that change is about to follow. The process of change can, however, be a lengthy and confused one. It is the obligation of people committed to change to hasten the collapse of the structures of oppression.

The church in defiance

With many political leaders imprisoned, detained, restricted or driven into exile, certain religious leaders have in recent years been thrust into media prominence. Churches acquired a measure of immunity from the effects of the state of emergency, and the structures and programmes of the churches and para-church organisations, together with the initiatives of Muslim and other religious groups, became viable vehicles for promoting the defiance campaign.

In the brief comment that follows a cursory attempt is made to identify the role of the churches in the defiance campaign, while recognising that with the release of political leaders from prison after 26 years and the imminent release of Nelson Mandela the role of church in the political struggle is set to change yet again.

The primary role of religious organisations is not political *per se.* It is rather to enable people to discern the liberating Spirit of God within the different dimensions of resistance and struggle – and to call people to join those organisations which promote justice and liberation. The *political* role which some religious leaders may acquire in the process of struggle can realistically only emerge as a result of popular and democratic support from the political organisations. The history of struggle in South Africa also shows that religious organisations (such as churches, mosques, synagogues and temples) and their leaders are encouraged to take their place alongside all other organisations in quest of a democratic future.

The aims and the tactics of the defiance campaign were clearly enunciated by MDM leadership at the beginning of August 1989: 'This is to be a peaceful programme of non-violent mass action, directed against apartheid laws and addressing the immediate needs and demands of our people.' Christians committed to the struggle for liberation·through churches that have repeatedly expressed concern about the resort to revolutionary violence responded positively, participating in the defiance campaign in a variety of different ways. These ranged from participation in protests against beach apartheid in Cape Town, Port Elizabeth and Durban to bus defiance in Pretoria, protests against segregation in provincial hospitals and massive city marches in Durban, East London, Johannesburg, Pietermaritzburg, Port Elizabeth, Pretoria and elsewhere. These were complemented by (in some cases proportionately even bigger) marches and rallies in rural towns like Beaufort West, Grabouw, George, Oudtshoorn, Uitenhage, Umtata, Worcester and similar size places.

At least part of this defiance (and especially the marches) were precipitated by defiance activities leading to the first 'legal' march that took place in Cape Town. The comment that follows focuses on these events in Cape Town, but only with a view to providing insight into the kind of resistance and defiance in which Christians and others shared in various parts of the country.

Parables of resistance

'Those who struggle for truth to triumph over lies, peace over violence, justice over injustice and liberation over oppression can be sure that God is on their side,' said Frank Chikane, General Secretary of the South African Council of Churches, at the conclusion of the Peace March on 13 September in Cape Town called by Archbishop Desmond Tutu and Dr Allan Boesak. 'I come from Soweto, but God is in the western Cape,' quipped Chikane, as he addressed the huge crowd participating in the Peace March, estimated at more than 30 000 people. 'What has happened here today', he said, 'can never be stopped.'

Certainly the march was a turning point in the struggle. It was the first legal event of its kind since the declaration of the state of emergency in 1985, and the biggest march since the one led by the young Philip Kgosana, shortly before the banning of the African National Congress (ANC) and Pan-Africanist Congress (PAC) on 8 April 1960 – events discussed in Chapter 2.

Three Cape Town events serve as parables that highlight the pathos and euphoria of the struggle *of* the church's engagement in the struggle (but also *for* the church as an ally in the struggle).

March on parliament

The church's Standing for the Truth Campaign got off to a tardy start half way through 1988 when representatives of the South African Council of Churches (SACC), the Southern African Cath-

olic Bishops' Conference (SACBC), African Independent Churches and Christians from some other groupings met in Johannesburg to plan a programme of non-violent action against apartheid.
It was the general call for defiance by the MDM that injected it with
a sense of purpose and direction. The days leading up to the
apartheid elections of 6 September saw the Standing for the Truth
Campaign in Cape Town at the forefront of protest and resistance.
Pickets, marches, meetings, women's action, the distribution of
pamphlets and other acts of defiance had Christians and others
arrested, beaten and detained. The events came to a climax with a
march on parliament on 2 September.

The city was under seige. Aproximately 1000 people were arrested. People were knocked down by riot police and beaten, others
were whipped and hundreds dispersed with the infamous purple-
dye water cannon. Ordinary, apolitical, non-engaged Capetonians
were outraged at the police being allowed to run amok in the city
– although they have got away with similar and far worse action in
the townships for years.

All kinds of people were brought together in Caledon Square
police station, in the kind of solidarity that only a police or prison
cell can produce: young and old, black and white, Christians,
Muslims, Jews and Hindus, Marxists, atheists, agnostics, profes-
sional people, workers, lawyers, clerics, business people, hawkers,
school children and unemployed.

The engagement of Christians in the defiance campaign must
first of all be understood at this level. The majority of people within
the church are black and as such victims of the apartheid system.
In the ground-swell of resistance that has been seen in the streets
of Cape Town, Christians should be expected to be demographi-
cally prominent. South Africans, and not least of all black South
Africans, are essentially a religious people. With political leadership
detained and imprisoned they demanded that priests, moulanas
and others take a lead in the resistance process. 'They have an
obligation to be caretakers until our leaders return,' said a young
comrade.

The church was obliged to be an actor in the social and political
context of revolution of which it is a part. Not all Christians were at
ease with this process and some responded to right-wing religious
initiatives and those conservative evangelical and mainline churches which distance themselves from the political turmoil. There
were, however, sufficient Christians (especially oppressed Chris-

tians) who were demanding that their churches reflect the spirit of people's defiance.

The right to worship God and resist evil

Two days after the march on parliament a rally organised by the Cape Democrats, an affiliate of the UDF, under the banner of 'Free and Fair Elections' was banned. The Central Methodist Mission responded by organising a service of worship and protest at the Buitenkant Street Methodist Church. The police insisted that the ban covered the church service as well, nailed the banning order to the door of the church and surrounded the building with Casspirs. Armed with teargas and quirts (sjamboks), police drove off people who came to worship.

The leaders of the Central Methodist Mission took the Commissioner of Police to the Supreme Court to have the banning order set aside. The argument of the security police was that church services of this kind were consistently being used as a guise to promote illegal political goals. Eventually the judged ruled. 'I am not prepared to ban a church service, if indeed it is a church service,' he said. At eleven o' clock that night the Casspirs were withdrawn, the police went home, the doors of the church were opened and Christians and others claimed the right to worship God and resist evil. The service ended with the singing of the national anthem, *Nkosi Sikelel' iAfrika,* at midnight. The most determined attempt to date by the state to eliminate the space opened up in the churches for resistance under the state of emergency, had been defeated.

As the demands of the new society begin to be felt within the institutional church, some Christians (but certainly not all) are beginning to realise that it is in *their* interest to change. A trusted elder statesperson in the church who accepts the responsibility of the church to be a vehicle of resistance at this point of South African history, observed recently, 'I long for the day when we can return to ecclesial normality!'

The peace march

The night following the court victory saw the killing of almost 30 people in the 'coloured' and black townships of Cape Town. Police brutality reached a level not seen in recent history. Then came the peace march. The state was forced to allow it to go ahead, and MDM spokespersons Archbishop Tutu, Allan Boesak and Frank Chikane addressed the crowd from the balcony of the city hall festooned with the flag of the African National Congress. 'It is hard to believe that ten days ago we were beaten and jailed in this city for doing less than we did today,' said one of the organisers. 'We are a new people, a rainbow people, marching to freedom,' said Tutu. 'Mr De Klerk, if you know what is good for you, join us in this struggle for a new South Africa. We are unstoppable.'

But the heady celebrations of the day were spiked with realism. 'Resistance will continue,' said Boesak. 'It will continue until the state of emergency is lifted, until detentions are no more, until schools are free of a police presence, until Nelson Mandela and others are out of prison, until unjust laws are removed from the statute books, until all South Africans are eligible to vote, until South Africa is free.'

The significance of the Cape Town march was not lost on the rest of the country and within the weeks that followed similar marches were held in all the major cities and several rural areas. ANC flags were openly displayed and there is little doubt in anyone's mind of the extent of the support for the liberation movement. The impact was not lost on the government, pressure was being applied on international banks not to roll-over South Africa's loans and demand for further sanctions against South Africa was high on the agenda.

The newly elected De Klerk government was forced to act. He announced that eight top political leaders would be unconditionally released from prison. Walter Sisulu, Ahmed Kathrada, Wilton Mkwayi, Elias Motsoaledi, Raymond Mhlaba, Andrew Mlangeni and Oscar Mpetha – all top ANC leadership – and Japhta Masemola, sentenced for PAC activities, were released in the early hours of the morning of 15 October, to join Govan Mbeki released on 5 November 1987.

Caught up in the struggle, the church has had the gospel of resistance and liberation proclaimed to it by the oppressed and repressed masses of South Africa. A careful consideration of theological themes considered in Parts Two and Three of this book suggests that the church is obliged actively to share in the struggle for a new South Africa.

December 1989

Acknowledgements

Chapters 3 and 4 of this book were first delivered as the Carl Christian Hein Lectures at four Lutheran seminaries in the United States of America in April 1988: Trinity Lutheran Seminary, Columbus, Ohio; Lutheran Northwestern Theological Seminary, St Paul, Minnesota; Wartburg Theological Seminary, Dubuque, Iowa; and Pacific Lutheran Seminary, Berkeley, California. Chapter 5 was a lecture in the Distinguished South African Lectures series at Georgetown University in October 1987, and subsequently published under the title 'Theology, Law and State Illegitimacy: An Agenda for Theology and Lawyers,' in the *Journal of Law and Theology*, 5, 2, 1987 and the *Journal of Theology for Southern Africa*, Number 63, June 1988. Chapter 6 was delivered as a paper at a conference in Princeton, New Jersey, in October 1988, organised by the Theology in Global Context Association. All this material has been substantially revised for publication in its present form.

I am grateful to those who made these lectures possible and to those who in their responses to the papers contributed to the final published form. During these visits many old friendships were renewed and new friends made: Jack de Gioia, Dean of Students at Georgetown University; Wynne Stumme at Trinity Lutheran Seminary in Columbus, Ohio; Paul Hanson, whom I met at Luther Northwestern Seminary; and Tshenuwani Farisani, an old and trusted friend, tortured in South African prisons, and presently a visiting scholar at the Pacific Lutheran Theological Seminary, where he lives in exile. Ed Huenemann, director of the Theology in Global Context Association, who has never tired of showing the significance of classical theological debate for contextual issues, assisted in coordinating my visit. Allan Boesak, initially invited to deliver the Hein lectures, proposed that I be the 1988 Hein lecturer. After consideration, the invitation was extended by the Division of Ministry of the Evangelical Lutheran Church in America, in consultation with the presidents of the four seminaries concerned.

Colleagues in the Department of Religious Studies at the University of Cape Town have contributed in discussion and debate to my theology and understanding of the social function of religion in society. The Institute for Contextual Theology has provided a space within which to explore and debate theology that engages and confronts apartheid. Mary Armour, a graduate student and skilled editorial assistant, facilitated the production of the manuscript for publication. Pat Lawrence, departmental administrative assistant, has the most remarkable ability to hunt down the most obstinately hidden pieces of information. To all these people I express my thanks. I am also grateful to David Philip in South Africa and Bill Eerdmans in the United States for agreeing to publish this book.

To acknowledge the support of one's family after the long process of writing is complete is always necessary and most sincerely given. To Eileen, Heidi and Tanya I am grateful.

Abbreviations

AMWU	African Mine Workers' Union
ANC	African National Congress
APO	African Political (*later* People's) Organisation
AZACTU	Azanian Confederation of Trade Unions
AZAPO	Azanian People's Organisation
BPC	Black People's Congress
CNETU	Council for Non-European Trade Unions
COSATU	Congress of South African Trade Unions
CUSA	Council of Unions of South Africa
CYL	Congress Youth League of the ANC
DPSC	Detainees' Parents Support Committee
ECC	End Conscription Campaign
FOSATU	Federation of South African Churches
FSAW (*later* FEDSAW)	Federation of South African Women
ICU	Industrial and Commercial Workers' Union
JMC	Joint Management Centre
LMC	Local Management Committee
LMS	London Missionary Society
LWF	Lutheran World Federation
NACTU	National Council of Trade Unions
NEUM	Non-European (*later* New) Unity Movement
NSMS	National Security Management System
NUM	National Union of Mineworkers
PAC	Pan-Africanist Congress
SACC	South African Council of Churches
SACP	South African Communist Party

SACPO	South African Coloured People's Organisation
SACTU	South African Congress of Trade Unions
SAIC	South African Indian Congress
SANC	South African Native Congress
SANNC	South African Native National Congress
SASO	South African Students' Organisation
SSC	State Security Council
UDF	United Democratic Front
UWCO	United Women's Congress
WARC	World Alliance of Reformed Churches
WCC	World Council of Churches

Introduction

Civil disobedience, revolutionary violence and illegitimate government have emerged as the major issues on the contemporary theological agenda of the church in South Africa. These issues, first set out in an explicit manner in the *Kairos Document* published in 1985, constitute the theological foci of this book.

From the time of the Edict of Milan in 313 C. E. the institutional church has traditionally been located on the side of successive ruling classes. This has resulted in the dominant theological tradition of the church insisting that the issues addressed here (civil disobedience, violence and the denunciation of illegitimate government) are to be considered only as a *last resort*. The moderate character of the Christian faith makes historical analysis, as a means of enquiring whether other options have been tried prior to resorting to the more drastic actions, an inherent and necessary part of serious theological debate. Its moderation also allows, however, that where cautious options for resistance fail to bring about justice, or are simply excluded as possibilities by the repression of the state, the church is obliged to engage in more radical means in the execution of its mandate, which is to ensure the liberty of God's children here on earth.

The nexus between critical theology and the history of struggle provides an opportunity for the rediscovery of the liberative resources of traditional theology. The neglect and disregard of this nexus by theologians of the dominant classes have too often removed theology from the political agenda of society, relegating it to the realm of abstraction and social irrelevancy.

Differently stated, the concern to know the will of God in a given situation can never be divorced from, or promoted as a substitute for, a thorough knowledge of the real world. 'An error about the world redounds in error about God,' wrote St. Thomas Aquinas.[1] Leonardo and Clodovis Boff insist that while the prime object of theology is God, before asking what oppression means in God's eyes theologians must ask the more basic question about the actual socio-political and economic nature of oppression and its causes.[2] Only against the historical reality of actual exploitation and suffering in a given place at a given time can serious theological debate happen.

In what follows, the social location of the church within the present South African crisis is explicitly acknowledged as a basis for determining the theo-political urgency with which debate on the issues already identified must be pursued. Discussion within the church of the oppressed on these issues has moved beyond the confines of academic debate. If theological debate is to have any significance at all in the South African situation, it must be pertinent to the historical and prevailing situation of oppression in this country. The pages that follow constitute a deliberate rejection of that theology which fails to emerge from the heat of the actual resistance. The intention is to reclaim the traditional theological resources of the church for the purpose of spiritual, cultural, political and socio-economic renewal. As such, the character of the theology in the second and third parts of this book is deliberately 'traditional', seeking to show that when renewed by the relevant questions posed by contextual theological debate, 'traditional theology' complements 'liberation theology' in renewing both church and society. Conversely, when theology is used as a basis for legitimating an unjust social order and exacting obedience to tyrannical rulers, or as a means of denying the right of an oppressed and suffering people to resort to arms without providing an alternative means to liberation, such theologising becomes an instrument of oppression.

Living between the times

South Africa, it can justifiably be argued, is presently in a period of its history within which, to quote Antonio Gramsci, 'the old is dying and the new cannot be born'.[3] What should be the role of the church in this interregnum? But this question loses its *kairos* meaning if it is not realised that the church itself (no less than the state) requires radical renewal. The church needs to discover what it means theologically to 'live between the times' if it is to share in the process of political renewal. It needs also to realise that it is historically not well-equipped to do so.

Barth wrestled with this question in Hitler's Germany in the

1930s, but the Confessing Church lost its impetus after the collapse of Nazism. The Confessing Church consisted, argued Hans Jochen Margull, of a diverse conglomerate of heterogeneous individuals bound together primarily by the need to counter a common enemy. Then, when Hitler no longer rendered the church this service, it collapsed and was absorbed into the all-encompassing structures of a new brand of liberal Christianity.[4] The institutional churches in many parts of Africa, in nations ranging from Ghana, which obtained its independence in 1957, to Zimbabwe, which became independent in 1980, also showed the promise of new life on the eve of independence. Before long, however, they too tumbled into the comfort of their own brand of Constantinian captivity. Churches of the Third World, unable to escape the missionary mode of existence, often reflect values in newly emerged nations that are not very different from those affirmed under colonialism. Frequently their religio-cultural conservatism hinders newly independent nations in their quest to throw off the last vestiges of the colonial past. Indeed, the role of the different churches in Third World revolutionary and post-revolutionary situations like Nicaragua, the Philippines, Angola, Mozambique and Zimbabwe is politically ambiguous, requiring serious theological review.

New wine requires new wine skins. Optimistically the Bible speaks of the potency of the new wine being capable of destroying the old skins. Often, however, so rigid, tough and enduring are the old skins that they sour and ultimately destroy the vitality of the new wine.

Despite the ambiguity of the social and political role of the institutional church, its theology allows traditionally for a sense of human restlessness which instinctively rebels against all forms of oppression and repression. This theology of resistance, hidden within even the most submissive and accommodating of theological formulations, has been identified elsewhere.[5] Johan Baptist Metz refers to it as the 'dangerous memory' of the gospel which simply cannot be ignored.[6] It is a theological 'given' which ultimately makes the church an uneasy accomplice in any social or political alliance that does not function in the interests of the poor and the oppressed.

The church is obliged to respond to the revolutionary cry found in all oppressive societies. This cry is, however, often confused and ambiguous, muffled and manipulated by the oppressor. The theological task of the church is therefore also to discern and interpret this cry when others ignore it (Luke 10: 25–37), proclaiming it with a boldness that cannot be misunderstood or disregarded. In order for this to happen the church must ensure that the ambiguity of resistance should not be allowed to conceal the anguish of the oppressed or their determination to be free.

The ambiguity of dependence

The interplay between the poles of collaboration and resistance among oppressed people is often more complex than would appear to be the case. It is a complexity referred to by Shula Marks as 'the ambiguities of dependence'.[7] Societies engaged in resistance or collaboration, in fact, have more in common with one another than is often realised.[8]

The complex range of responses to colonisation (and few subjugated societies have not engaged in both accommodation and resistance) is often determined as much by opportunity, internal organisation and social structure as it is by deliberate ideological choice. Adaptation and submission among small and vulnerable societies are options never easily denied. Yet even in the most vulnerable and submissive societies resistance remains just below the surface, emerging sometimes only in isolated, covert and passive forms. This pattern is seen in the history of resistance in South Africa considered in Chapters 1 and 2. History also shows, however, that when such options are exhausted resistance invariably intensifies. It acquires an organisational character, and revolution becomes inevitable.

Karl Marx was correct in predicting the inevitability of revolution and violence in certain situations. Commenting on emergent Russian terror in 1881, he saw violence as a historically inevitable means of action, 'the morality or immorality of which', he suggested, 'is as useless to discuss as that of the earthquake at Chios.'[9] In reality, however, revolution invariably emerges only after other less dramatic options have been exhausted, showing the theological teaching on the 'last resort' to be not only a necessary but realistic dictum rather than a piece of romantic idealism. To quote Fatima Meer, 'Revolution, though dependent on the populace, is not a popular cause. The security of a familiar system, even if limiting, is invariably preferable to the risks of change.'[10] Equally true, however, is the observation of Selby Msimang, an official of the black Industrial and Commercial Workers' Union founded in 1919. He discerned the theological essence of resistance in saying, 'Man is not bound to confess loyalty to the tyrant. History has shown that the human soul naturally revolts against injustice.'[11]

Preoccupation with revolution often, however, results in the historical and theological neglect of important but unsung alternative forms of resistance which do not produce immediate transformation of the social order. In situations of extreme repression such tactics are frequently as heroic as the more spectacular acts of revolution, and often represent the only avenue of resistance open to the oppressed.

This raises the question concerning the distinction between wanton criminality and popular rebellion. In their history of crime in eighteenth-century England, the authors of *Albion's Fatal Tree* initially made a distinction between two kinds of offence and offenders. They identified as 'good criminals', those whom they saw as premature revolutionaries or reformers, the forerunners of popular movements. The other group they described as being 'committed to crime without qualification', or 'indiscriminate criminals'. As they progressed in their analysis, however, the two categories of offenders collapsed into one another. Both groups were often guilty of the same kind of offences and suffered the same kind of punishment from the authorities. There was also no clear evidence that the community was more or less inclined to protect one kind of offender from the law in preference to the other, and both groups responded with equal brutality to those who threatened to betray them.[12] Whatever the intention, the diffuse behavioural patterns of the oppressed were seen to weld into a broad-based politics of discontent and resistance. Certainly the response of the oppressed, particularly in the early period of colonisation in South Africa discussed in Chapter 1, shows precisely this kind of complexity. Reinhold Niebuhr once observed that grace and ambition are intertwined, giving expression to the greatness and weakness of humankind.[13] It may well be said that in oppressive societies 'criminality' and resistance together contribute to the seething discontent that makes for a revolutionary climate.

'Resistance studies', as a relatively new phenomenon in South African historiography, reveal the intensity and inventiveness of the political resistance of the oppressed. They also belie the myth of a lack of response on the part of the indigenous populace to white hegemony – a peaceful acceptance said to be disturbed only by a few instigators. Studies of resistance also make total nonsense of the judgment of those who suggest that the oppressed people of South

Africa have engaged in organised non-violent action for only a fleeting eight years between the Defiance Campaign in 1952 and the time when the African National Congress (ANC), and the Pan-Africanist Congress (PAC) were banned in 1960.[14] The memory of a long and enduring history of struggle and resistance by former generations functions as a disturbing incentive among today's oppressed. When this is related to the 'dangerous memory' of the gospel the church becomes the locus of restlessness and struggle. In turn, the possibility of theological engagement with and in the social revolution becomes a reality.

The history of political struggle reaches back to the earliest encounters between black and white in South Africa. This early resistance included slave rebellions, raids undertaken by warriors and guerilla groups, the defiance of the ravaged Khoisan people, the desperate struggle for survival among the Griqua, and wars fought by established chiefdoms on the margins of the ever-shifting frontiers of land occupied by whites. It was manifest in heroic and inventive non-violent actions by the oppressed, as well as courageous armed struggle by chiefdoms which had once ruled over the land with unquestioned authority. It erupted among peasants, the petite-bourgeoisie, intellectuals, government-appointed headmen, women, students, industrial workers, shebeen queens, ministers of religion, and an impoverished proletariat who clung to the fringes of the new urban and industrial areas. It incorporated rural as well as urban constituencies, and often crystallised around local community issues and seemingly apolitical events, sometimes dismissed by historians as evidence of social irresponsibility and unqualified criminality. These events ranged from trading disagreements, agricultural campaigns, the right of local women to brew beer, rumours that shops were selling poisoned goods, and religious schisms to food boycotts in schools and resistance to mission education. All important ingredients in a resistance culture (within which the divide between cause and effect becomes blurred), these events provide important insights into the character and the extent of resistance.

The limited ways in which the masses have been constrained to contest the terms of their subordination have made as important a contribution to the history of struggle in South Africa as the high profile frontier and occupational wars accentuated in the popular histories of white domination. These limited resistance campaigns have contributed significantly to what Beinart and Bundy have

identified as 'the nascent urban–rural alliances ... rudely inter-
rupted by the banning of the ANC and the PAC in 1960, and by the
repressive force of the state's response to their underground activities.'[15]

History as a theological hermeneutic

In Chapter 1 an attempt is made to provide an insight into the early
broad-based and varied forms of resistance that constitute the
historical background to the more intense, better organised and
overtly revolutionary character of resistance in South Africa which
emerged largely in response to the racism inherent in the constitution of the Union of South Africa, declared in 1910, and in the 1913
Natives Land Act. This latter form of resistance, considered in
Chapter 2, can be adequately understood only in relation to the
more hesitant and cautious actions of earlier times. The more
radical responses constitute a 'last resort' by the oppressed in
asserting their unquestionable right to be free. It is this hermeneutic which underlies the theological debate in Chapters 3, 4 and
5, as it does in Chapter 6, in which the identity and responsibility
of the church within the present situation are discussed.

In seeking to provide an insight into the history of struggle as a
basis for engaging in serious theological debate, the writer makes
no claim to be a historian. Chapters 1 and 2 are intended merely
to ground theology in a specific historical context. They function
as a *hermeneutic reminder*, meant to prevent theological debate from
degenerating into abstract theory quite unrelated to reality. Details
on battles fought, agreements reached and treaties broken are not
provided here. Nor are all the contours of the long history of
oppression, established through blood and conflict, considered.
The historical detail that is provided is meant only to identify and
explain particular manifestations of resistance – as a contextual
basis for addressing *theological* issues in subsequent chapters.

In this sense the book provides a deliberately selective historical
insight, intended to draw attention to the process of resistance
often overlooked or deliberately excluded from some popular
histories of South Africa. Because of the theological character of
this publication attention is also given to the ambiguous role of
religion in the resistance struggle, without any attempt being made
to develop systematically the character or social function of religion
in society.

The burden of the past weighs heavily on present activity. People make their own history, but do not make it under circumstances chosen by themselves. They do so 'under circumstances directly encountered, given and transmitted from the past.' 'The tradition of all dead generations', Marx reminds us, 'weighs like a nightmare on the brain of the living.'[16] Often it is the tradition of the strong and the powerful, those who ordinarily have time to write history, the victors, that weighs most heavily on the oppressed. For theology to be done from the perspective of the poor and the oppressed this dominant interpretation must be corrected or even destroyed. History has to be rewritten and reappropriated as a liberating instrument within the hands of the victims of a history of subjugation. In order for this to happen, the stories of resistance, the songs of liberation, and the myths and dreams of the subjugated need to be rediscovered and retold.

To identify the spirit of God within the struggle of a people is always a risky business, and history is cluttered with the wreckage of nations and people who have reduced the will of God to their own political accomplishments. The best that any people can achieve is necessarily less than the ultimate will of God, and it is argued in the pages that follow that this theological imperative constitutes a political ingredient which ought not to be neglected. It provides a necessary critique of revolution that undermines the temptation to sanctify any particular political order. The church, we argue, is obliged to serve the cause of the poor and oppressed in each successive age. This means that its alliances may change from one generation to another, but this should never distract from its obligation to serve those who are poor and oppressed *now*.

Correctly understood, the most radical form of theo-political engagement in the struggle for justice necessarily affirms a position of 'permanent revolution' – in which all political solutions are constantly renewed in the interests of those who suffer most. 'Grace', says Karl Barth, 'means divine impatience, discontent, dissatisfaction: it means that the whole is required. Grace is the enemy of everything, even of the most indispensable "interim ethic". Grace is the axe laid at the root of the good conscience which the politician and the civil servant always wish to enjoy....'[17]

This 'negative critique' of the political order can never, however, be an excuse for failing to discern the 'positive' presence of the spirit of God in history at the present time. When Christians are fired by the great hope of a new age (the *eschaton*), the signs of God's presence in the smaller victories and revolutions can be discerned.[18]

The stories of God's revelation in the Old Testament are stories which seem to suggest that God's people are little by little discerning who God is and where God is to be found. The New Testament is *inter alia* an account of believers discovering anew who God is, under different circumstances. Similarly, Christians are today also required to learn continually where God is within each new situation in which they find themselves. The spirit of resistance and the continuing quest by oppressed people for their God-given right to be free provide fertile conditions for discerning the spirit of God. God can never be reduced to the human spirit of resistance and the demand to be free, but neither is God less than that. Where freedom, hope and liberation are struggling to be born, Christians are theologically required to acknowledge the presence of God.

To recognise God in the history of struggle in South Africa is an exercise which liberates those engaged in the contemporary pursuit of justice and helps them draw strength from an enduring history of struggle engaged in by former generations. This is a history within which there are signs of the presence of the spirit of God. Speaking at the conclusion of a meeting between South Africans and Palestinians in Jerusalem in January 1989, Malusi Mpumlwana said:

When I hear the story of the Intifada, I say 'amen'. This is part of the same process as the one which we have in South Africa. The same spirit that is moving people here is moving people in the resistance movement in South Africa.

Our people have been dispossessed. They have been kept uneducated all these years. In spite of all this, they have been able to rise…. This experience says to me, that God can never be defeated, that is a sign of hope.[19]

The ethics of last resort

In traditional theology resistance is directly related to the formative argument of *last resort*. This argument forms an important restraining consideration that seeks to limit war and armed rebellion. The story of the crusades and politically inspired holy wars of revenge, which have marred the history of the church, are enough to convince Christians of the place of an ethics of last resort in developing a theo-political understanding of resistance and rebellion. This ethic should not, however, be used to constrain other ongoing forms of political participation by the church, on the ground that the church is only in exceptional situations – as a last resort – required to act politically. Should it act in situations of crisis only as a 'last resort', its contribution usually comes too late. By that time other history-making forces have already irreversibly shaped the future.[20]

This kind of passivity, which has come to characterise some manifestations of the Christian religion, has no place in a theology of social renewal. It is quite wrong to assume that 'good law' or 'legitimate government' is God-given in the sense of a Platonic ideal type, and allow that civil disobedience and questions of illegitimate government are appropriate only where the state is judged to have transgressed these limits of authority. Judicial laws and notions of legitimate rule are not once-given divine gifts, but historically constructed realities which function as social instruments to regulate and order society. In order for people to engage seriously in the formation of law, civil disobedience and questions of illegitimate rule ought to be consistently considered as normative options on an on-going basis – and not be reserved only for extreme or *Grenzfall* situations.

Classical notions of law and legitimate rule are dependent on arguments of moral and theological legitimacy, but such notions are generally not relied on as a legitimating basis for contemporary secular society. Above all, in a national security state – a form of government that has found powerful support in even the established democracies of the world – the structures of moral persuasion have given way to militaristic and technological mechanisms of survival and repression.[21] In such situations, where public debate is manipulated, if not totally controlled, and democracy reduced to little more than a cover for dictatorial rule, it can justifiably be argued that civil disobedience, political non-cooperation and the rejection of state authority as illegitimate are the *only* appropriate actions available. And some will argue that in contemporary society, where classical theological forms of judicial and state legitimation no longer operate, an ethics of last resort is no longer valid.

Pertinent as this argument may be, few states fail to seek some form of moral or religious legitimation, however superficial, for their existence and behaviour. This much is clear from the preambles to many state constitutions (such as the preamble to the South African constitution), and from the civil religion generated around public events, while religious ideology and moral rhetoric are an important part of most national security ideologies. Without overestimating the importance of any form of moral argument in the sphere of politics, the theological and moral questioning (and denunciation) of a state's legitimation structure can constitute a modest but important *political* exercise. If the focus of one's concern is futhermore the mobilisation of the Christian church, traditional theological arguments – questioned and inwardly renewed in order to face the challenge of contemporary demands – are persuasive spiritual and political levers not to be neglected.

The whirlwind

Friedrich Nietzsche has articulated better than most the rebellion of the oppressed against dominant forms of morality, theological obscuration and historiography written from the perspective of those who benefit most from the maintenance of the existing order: 'As long as your morality hung over me I breathed like one asphyxiated [he observed]. That is why I throttled this snake. I wished to live. Consequently it had to die.'[22]

Nietzsche dismissed Christianity (more correctly, the ruling-class Christianity as interpreted in the nineteenth-century Prussian state) as a 'slave morality', employed by the rich and powerful to keep the poor and oppressed in subjection. Karl Barth spoke of this morality as a 'morality … that turns out to be a lie'. It involves the construction of a theology and a morality which exalt our own requirements, to which we demand that God must adjust Godself. It involves the powerful and dominant people of both church and society creating a 'God' whose values are their own values, a 'God' who is ultimately their private possession. The result is a blind, uncritical and capricious system of thought and behaviour, protected by a false piety which Barth simply calls 'the Night'. 'The revolt of Prometheus is wholly justified once Zeus – the "No-God" – has been exalted to the throne,' he continues. In this situation, Barth remarks, we are obliged to remember that 'the speech of God can always be heard out of the whirlwind'.[23] In situations of oppression and rebellion around the world, where the whirlwind of rebellion is raging, the speech of God is being heard anew. Theology is being renewed among the poor and oppressed who are in rebellion against oppressive structures and tyrants. This theology of oppressed people must, in turn, renew systems of morality and ecclesial theologies that make allowance for neither the place of 'ongoing revolution' in post-revolutionary situations nor the Promethean act of rebellion in oppressive situations.

Oppressed Christians today recognise that theology and morality, used by the oppressor to constrain and pacify the oppressed, are a distortion of the religion of the poor man of Nazareth who proclaimed a message of good news to the poor, liberty to the captive, recovery of sight to the blind, freedom for the oppressed and the jubilee year of the Lord (Luke 4: 18–19). Christianity which oppresses must die in order that Christianity which liberates may live.

PART ONE

Historical context

1
Early resistance

The encounter between black and white in South Africa has generated a history of fear, conflict, suspicion, intrigue, war, resistance, and ultimately black subjugation. It has been a long and intense encounter that began 500 years ago – and the struggle continues. The primary objectives of neither the oppressor nor the oppressed have yet been realised.

In this chapter an attempt is made to identify a tradition of black resistance that has countered every aspect of the white colonising process. It covers the period extending from the time of the first encounters between white explorers and the indigenous people to the establishment of the Union of South Africa in 1910, which entrenched white domination.

Early resistance was characterised by a long series of wars which eventually resulted in the reduction of the African population to proletarian status. It also included peasant non-cooperation, protest and defiance of a less evident kind. No people known to historians, suggests E. P. Thompson, has ever been exploited without finding some way of fighting back.[1] These acts of peasant and proletarian resistance in South Africa frequently had limited objectives, but collectively resulted in a permanent sense of unrest and latent revolution.

The institutional church, slow and reluctant to become involved in the resistance process, was often drawn into the counter-revolutionary activities of colonial and settler groups. The missionaries proclaimed a gospel that could scarcely be distinguished from the basic values of British imperialism, and 'conversion' in many instances became the 'psychological basis for a politics of colonialism'.[2]

Historical divisions are usually arbitrarily imposed and no attempt is made here to separate events prior to 1910 from those that followed that fateful year. The divide between chapters is rather between those acts of resistance that emerged as a result of the military defeat of the indigenous people (which are considered in Chapter 1), and such events as can be attributed to the emergence of political organisations which mushroomed after 1910 and shaped the character of twentieth-century resistance. These latter events are considered in Chapter 2. The different patterns of Khoisan, Griqua and African resistance are also not discussed in strict chronological order.

From a contented and peaceful people

It is historically neither helpful nor correct to blame all the woes of the indigenous people on the arrival of white settlers on the southern tip of Africa. The observation of a Stellenbosch landdrost in 1705 nevertheless provides an adequate summary of the effects of the colonisation process on the earliest inhabitants of the region: 'from a contented people peacefully supporting themselves with their cattle, [the Khoisan] have mostly all been changed into *bushmen* hunters and robbers, scattering everywhere among the mountains.'[3]

The earliest encounters between blacks and whites in South Africa seemed to mirror the kind of oppressive interaction that would endure for generations to come. Terrified by the pale apparitions from the sea, Khoikhoi herders who witnessed the landing of the Portuguese navigator Bartolomeu Dias and his mariners at Mossel Bay in 1488 hastily drove their cattle inland. Vasco da Gama, who landed at St Helena Bay in 1497, initially met with a friendly response from Khoikhoi in the area, but the encounter soon turned sour and he and wounded members of his party were obliged to escape back to their ships. Sailing further, they reached Mossel Bay and reported meeting a native people who rode on cattle, played flutes, danced and wore ivory armlets. Antonio de Saldanha, who sailed into Table Bay in 1503, was ambushed and wounded, and when Francisco d'Almeida (the first Portuguese viceroy in India) dropped anchor in Table Bay en route home in 1510, his fate was more serious. Having decided to punish a group of Khoikhoi for their treatment of mariners sent ashore to barter for food, the viceroy and 49 others were killed.[4]

The Cape sea-route to India was in time plied on a regular basis by English and Dutch commercial fleets which regularly dropped anchor in Table Bay. Their trade with the Khoikhoi (iron barrel-hoops and nails for cattle and sheep) began cautiously and with mutual suspicion, but soon degenerated into plunder.[5]

The early sporadic encounters eventually gave way to colonisation, which began with the establishment of a refuelling station by the Dutch East India Company (DEIC) in 1652. Little regard was shown for the social structure of the native people, and their unwillingness to part with large numbers of livestock was interpreted as open hostility, providing an excuse for reprisals.[6] Impatient with the protocol of the barter and trade system, the colonists acquired their supplies by force. And when the cattle of the Khoikhoi in the immediate vicinity of the Cape settlement were depleted, despite restrictions imposed by the DEIC, the colonists steadily began to possess the cattle of communities located further inland.

Slave defiance

Under strict instructions not to enslave the indigenous population, Van Riebeeck (the first DEIC governor) waited six years for the first consignment of slaves to arrive on the *Amersfoort,* but soon further shipments arrived from countries as diverse as West Africa, Mozambique, Madagascar, present-day Java, Bali, Timor, the Malayan peninsula, China and various parts of India. This heterogeneity worked against the emergence of slave unity, and was further complicated by class divisions between domestic slaves (who included artisans and craftspeople, permitted to hire out their skills) and the less privileged *akkerboer* (farm-labour) slaves. The judicial system dealt brutally with offending slaves. The slaves in response often brutalised one another and were divided among themselves. Under these circumstances, desertion seemed the only way out of their misery, and small runaway slave communities took refuge in mountainous and coastal hideaways.[7]

The resistance of slaves in the Cape was limited.[8] Despite the dreams of freedom that surfaced in the uprisings that did occur, successful rebellion was never a serious possibility. When the authorities introduced Ordinance 19 in June 1826, intended to limit the jurisdiction of slave owners over their slaves, the owners rose in revolt and attacked the property of several government officials in Stellenbosch.[9] It took until 1838 for slavery to be abolished, and this produced a howl of protest from Boer subsistence farmers. But colonial authorities, influenced by factors that shaped the Industrial Revolution in England, saw the economic future of the Cape in a different light. They anticipated the need for a pool of labour that could be drawn on or dismissed in accordance with the demands of production.[10]

Outnumbered, exploited and repressed, the slaves never presented a serious threat to the dominant position of whites. Other black people, however, *were* regarded as a threat, and the first serious conflicts with indigenous people came dangerously close to extermination. The Khoisan and the Griqua emerged from their encounter with colonial expansionism a depleted and savaged people.

Khoisan rebellion

The Khoisan (consisting of Khoikhoi herders and San hunter-gatherers) were a Late Stone Age people who already roamed the southern shores of Africa at the time of Christ. Their resistance to white colonisation from the seventeenth century onwards was both heroic and ambiguous. Ultimately it almost cost them their identity as a people.

The San doggedly resisted cultural assimilation and clung to the outer reaches of territory occupied by the white settlers. The Khoikhoi were more ready to engage with the settlers – both in trade and in war. And yet, suggests Shula Marks, 'there is little to distinguish a landless and cattleless Khoikhoi from a Bushman [San] who has acquired cattle from a Khoi.'[11] In brief, the shift from hunting and gathering to herding was not a once-and-for-all-time change, and when Khoikhoi land came under increased intrusion from the expanding settler community the Khoikhoi were obliged to revert to a hunter-gatherer lifestyle.

The story of the subjugation of the Khoikhoi essentially had to do with an insatiable demand for commodities. The settlers and the crews of ships passing around the Cape ravenously demanded fresh meat and other pastoral products. The Khoikhoi, in turn, developed an avid need for commodities which a pastoral economy could not provide. They wanted metal for trinkets, jewellery, arrowheads and assegais. 'Whole fleets', writes Elphick, 'could be fed in return for miscellaneous junk readily available on any ship.'[12] Within little more than sixty years after the arrival of Jan van Riebeeck at the Cape, the presence of European traders resulted in the total destruction of the centuries-old social and economic order of the Peninsular Khoikhoi. The final blow was inflicted by the 1713 smallpox epidemic. By the time the disease subsided the Khoi were a grossly diminished people.

When the herds of the Peninsular Khoikhoi were depleted,

trekboer 'hunting expeditions' and 'coercive trading' excursions were extended into the hinterland, and it has been suggested that 'at times it was difficult to distinguish ... cattle trading from ... raiding operations'.[13]

By the turn of the century the wealthiest of the Khoikhoi clans of the hinterland had also been robbed of their cattle, and the DEIC was obliged to allow 'free burghers' to enter the meat market. With this concession white encroachment onto Khoikhoi and Xhosa land further intensified.[14]

Khoikhoi subjugation did not, however, come about without a fight.[15] The first Khoi–Dutch war was fought as early as 1659–60, with victory evading the Goringhaiqua largely because of pressure from other Khoikhoi groups to allow trade with the Company to continue. The second Khoi–Dutch war came little more than a decade later (1673–77).[16] Eventually defeated in war, Khoikhoi resistance was seriously hindered by internal conflict, the lack of coordination between the different Khoikhoi groupings, drought, stock diseases and smallpox epidemics.[17] Often the only means of survival available to the depleted Khoikhoi was the raiding of white farms.

In the meantime the focus of confrontation had shifted to the eastern frontier of the white colony, where the settlers faced the more powerful Xhosa. And when the opportunity arose, the Khoisan joined the Xhosa in their wars of resistance. This was the case most notably in 1799–1802 when an uprising of Khoisan servants, who deserted from frontier farms with the guns and horses of their Boer masters, joined forces with the Xhosa in the third frontier war. The size of the desertion and the extent of the combined Xhosa–Khoisan uprising make this particular rebellion a significant focus for historians, but it was not the first time that Khoisan servants joined the resisters. Raids on the frontier farms rarely failed to include armed deserters.[18]

As suggested earlier, the divide between collaboration and resistance has never been clear-cut among the oppressed, and Khoisan resistance was manifest in desertion, the supplying of guns and ammunition to fugitives, murder, guerilla activity, migration to neighbouring clans, double-dealing and general 'lawlessness'.

Veldwagtmeesters (military overseers) were appointed from among the settlers, all males in the frontier districts were conscripted into the militia, and isolated outbreaks of guerilla activity thereafter diminished. The captured Khoisan were, in turn, used as indentured labour, and Khoisan children raised on Boer farms were obliged to work on the farm until at least the age of 18.[19]

London Missionary Society (LMS) missionaries tirelessly campaigned to improve the lot of the Khoikhoi. Their motives were, however, of a mixed kind. Dr John Philip, a political conservative and staunch advocate of middle-class British respectability, for example, argued that cordial treatment of the indigenous population was the surest way to ensure social stability and white hegemony.[20] And when Ordinance 50 was promulgated in 1828 (partly in response to missionary agitation), ostensibly freeing Khoisan servants from forced labour, the back of Khoisan resistance had already been broken. The Khoikhoi won a measure of freedom, but irrevocably lost their land.

Khoikhoi discontent continued well after 1828, as can be seen in the Kat River Rebellion, when the Khoikhoi inhabitants of the settlement used the eighth frontier war (which broke out on Christmas Day 1850) as their opportunity to rebel. The rebellion was crushed, the land of the rebels reallocated to whites, and soon whites were also able to buy up the remaining arable land on the settlement. The dream of an 'independent' settlement for Khoikhoi and freed slaves who had thus far survived settler aggression was soon little more than a memory.

Griqua defeat

Most of the Khoikhoi were driven into the service of whites, some were absorbed by the surrounding Tswana and Xhosa chiefdoms, while others re-established traditional links with scattered San communities. Still others, having intermarried with European settlers, were expelled from a society determined to preserve its white identity. In time these people of mixed race, together with groups of San, Khoikhoi, Namaqua and others, became a distinct people led by the Adam Koks, Barend and Nicholas Barends, the Waterboers and others. Called the 'Griqua' (in recognition of the Grigriqua or Khoikhoi part of their identity), they settled on LMS stations in the remote areas to the north of the Orange River, across the line of advancing trekboers.

Soon they were surrounded by Boer settlers, and in time the British extended the colonial border to the Orange River. Despite appeals by their leaders not to exchange ultimate security for immediate gain, the harassed Griqua were unable to resist the lure of goods, guns and liquor for the sale or exchange of land. Boer demand for land intensified and Adam Kok's comment to LMS missionary John Philip in 1831 expressed in a few words the fate of the hapless Griqua. 'We love freedom and fear the boers,' he said. Their only hope was to trek, but they 'knew not whither'.[21] A leadership struggle between Kok and the more capable Andries Waterboer (complicated by missionary support for the weaker Kok) further weakened Griqua resolve.

Not until thirty years later did the Griqua, now under Adam Kok III, abandon in 1861 what land they still occupied and trek for Nomansland (East Griqualand), while Waterboer and his followers remained in the area. Kok's move was, however, doomed before it began. His people received little compensation for their land and lost most of their stock in the trek through Basutoland, being left without the resources to pay even the registration fee for their new land allocations. Title deeds were often not issued, and white speculators managed to secure large blocks of farms. Kok's new state crumbled in much the same way as the first had done, and in 1879 the territory came under the direct rule of the Cape Colony.[22] Like Waterboer's followers, they too became servants, share-croppers and squatters on white-owned land.

In the meantime matters were also coming to a head in the Griqua territory north of the Orange River. The discovery of diamonds in 1867 intensified the scramble for the disputed land. An arbitration court honoured Griqua claims to the land (presented by Nicholaas Waterboer's agent and shrewd property dealer, David Arnot) but the award came too late to save Griqua independence. Waterboer was forced to offer his land to the Crown for protection and a few years later in 1880 it became part of the Cape Colony.

Racial divisions among diamond diggers effectively excluded the Griqua from sharing in the wealth of the diggings, and they lost their diamond claims together with what political influence they once had as a people. A new survey of the area showed that Waterboer's earlier claims were erroneous. The Orange Free State Republic reluctantly accepted 90 000 pounds sterling compensation for the land, and the British insisted that the territory was now their sole possession. The Griqua were reduced to the condition of a dependent proletariat.

Political success or barren victory?
The subjugation of the dominant African chiefdoms was achieved only after considerably greater resistance than either the Khoisan or the Griquas could muster. When 'victory' finally came to the settlers, it merely gave rise to a different kind of resistance that endures to the present times. The question posed by Bishop John Colenso after the defeat of the Zulu at Ulundi in 1879 could well be asked in relation to the subjugation of the African polities as a whole: 'Was it a political success,' he asked, 'or any more than a bloody but barren victory?'[23]

To understand the resistance of the major African chiefdoms it is necessary to reach back to the beginning of the nineteenth century. An all-engulfing struggle for power, known in Sotho as the *Difaqane* (hammering) and in the Nguni languages as the *Mfecane* (crushing), drastically altered the demography of the entire sub-continent. A political revolution which had started in what is today north-western Natal swept through the region, and soon affected virtually every chiefdom in southern Africa. Whatever the cause, the consequence was a domino effect of weaker groups and chief-doms being overrun or absorbed into the emerging dominant kingdom. While it left many of the indigenous people ill-equipped to resist white occupation of their territory, the victorious kingdoms became formidable opponents for Boer and Brit alike.

The second British occupation of the Cape in 1806 heralded a new phase in the interaction between blacks and whites in the area. Colonialism was at its height, missionary endeavour had become part of the imperialist dream, and the granting of land to British settlers along the eastern frontier of the colony throughout the 1820s meant that a new age had dawned on the African veld. The Xhosa on the eastern frontier had to be subdued, and this was undertaken in a more systematic and final way than anything the trekboers could possibly have hoped for or accomplished. But the Xhosa were defeated only after a long series of nine wars of dispossession, or frontier wars, in which the Xhosa defended their land at enormous cost. This story of white military might and Xhosa armed resistance has been told in many places and the details need not be repeated here. The story of the Great Trek, in which five thousand Voortrekkers (taking with them as many black servants) left the Cape Colony to escape British domination, to protest against the effects of the emancipation of slaves and to avoid the consequences which Ordinance 50 was having on their Khoisan labourers, is also too well-known to be repeated.

The Voortrekkers established independent Boer republics in Natal, the Transvaal and the Orange Free State; and in so doing fought, defeated and dominated black communities in much the same way as the British subdued the Xhosa on the eastern frontier of the Cape, the Zulu in Natal and the Pedi in the northern Transvaal. Ultimately the British and the Boers had only one another to fight and this they did on two successive occasions, in 1880–1 and again in 1899–1902.

The long campaign that resulted in the subjugation of the African chiefs began, however, a century earlier with the first encounter between white settlers and the Xhosa in the Zuurveld (a stretch of land between the Sundays and Great Fish rivers). It is here that our account of African resistance must begin.

The Xhosa, once a powerful nation, resisted white encroachment with every means at their disposal. They raided cattle (a typical mode of warfare), attacked white settlements, and where they cooperated with the settlers it was only to help resolve an internal conflict or as a temporary truce. Border skirmishes and wars were, in fact, to continue from before the first frontier war fought in 1779 for the next hundred years. These events, well-documented in many histories of the period, are discussed in what follows only to the extent that it is necessary to illustrate and explain the culture of resistance that emerged in the face of defeat and white domination. This culture was manifest in religious protests, struggles hidden within the structures and customs of rural society, agricultural protests, school boycotts, women's protests and armed rebellion.

Religion as protest

The church played an ambiguous role in African society throughout the colonial period. The missionaries actively promoted colonial advances made into African society and in some instances welcomed military aggression against the Xhosa and other chiefdoms. The defeat of African chiefs, the shattered morale of the people, the loss of land, the confiscation of cattle and the collapse of African culture created a milieu within which missionary attempts to lure Africans into their missions became that much easier.[24]

Initially rejected by the majority of African chiefs, missionary endeavours met with a measure of success only when the socio-economic, political and cultural structures of Xhosa society began to crumble in the wake of the frontier wars. To become a Christian was to become Westernised, to live in square houses, wear Western clothes and participate in the colonial economy.

The rejection of early missionary endeavours is most clearly seen in the response to the Christian message of two Xhosa diviners, Nxele and Ntsikana. Both their responses were born out of the heat of Xhosa reaction to colonisation, providing important precursors of two alternative types of religious resistance that emerged at regular intervals in the history of the black resistance struggle in South Africa.[25]

Ndlambe had been appointed regent of the Rharhabe, a dominant Xhosa sub-chiefdom living on the eastern frontier of the Cape Colony, to govern until the boy-king Ngqika (Gaika) was old enough. When Ndlambe became reluctant to surrender power, Ngqika turned against him and an internal power struggle followed. Things came to a head in 1811. Ndlambe and his followers together with all other Xhosa groups were driven out of the Zuurveld and into Ngqika's territory with ruthless efficiency by colonial and Boer forces under the command of Lieutenant-Colonel John Graham. 'I am happy to add', wrote the Governor of the Cape, Sir John Cradock, to the Home Office, 'that in the course of this service there has not been shed more Kaffir blood than would seem to be necessary to impress on the minds of these savages a proper degree of terror and respect.'[26]

During this period Nxele, a millenarian prophet and diviner in Ndlambe's household, had visions that favoured Ndlambe's military success and he quickly emerged as a major influence in Xhosa politics by conspiring with Ndlambe against the less popular and weaker Ngqika. Having turned against his missionary mentors, he taught his followers to sing as they went to war of the day when whites would be driven into the sea:

> To chase the White men from the Earth,
> And drive them to the sea.
> The sea that cast them up at first,
> For Ama Xhosa's curse and bane,
> Howls for the progeny she nursed
> To swallow them again.[27]

Ngqika was ousted in battle by Ndlambe and, despite being restored to power by the British, was defeated a second time. The

British again came to Ngqika's assistance and this time, at the instigation of Nxele, who promised that British bullets would be turned to water, Ndlambe attacked Graham's Town in 1819. Unable to withstand the British artillery, Ndlambe's 6 000 warriors were defeated and the Xhosa forced to acknowledge Ngqika as paramount chief. 'People say that I have occasioned this war,' Nxele is reported to have said. 'Let me see whether delivering myself up to my conquerors will restore peace to my country.' [28] He was sentenced to life imprisonment by the British, became an early political prisoner on Robben Island, and drowned trying to escape a while later.

What makes Nxele important in a study of resistance is his affirmation of a millenarian-type religious response to white domination which would emerge again and again in black resistance. Equally important in this regard is Ntsikana's religious response.[29] Less radical in his rejection of the missionaries' gospel, Ntsikana's message was as roundly condemned by the missionaries as had been the message of Nxele.

Ntsikana's religious views were probably shaped as much by the fact that he had been rejected by the more powerful Ndlambe, as they were by his sharing in Ngqika's forced accommodationist response to colonialism. He constantly warned against the dangers of Western ideas and sought to revive traditional Xhosa values, but in giving Xhosa values to Christian symbols in his hymns and ritualistic practices he enabled the Xhosa to identify with the emergent Christian and colonial milieu. This, as well as his counsel to Ngqika not to go to war against the settler community, has given rise to the inevitable question whether his brand of religion did not, like the religion of the missionaries, merely soften the blow of imperial subjugation. Yet in time it was this synthesis that gave rise to forms of resistance among the members of indigenous churches which were more radical and less compromising than Ntsikana's had ever been. 'Nxele was a wardoctor and his cosmology was one of battle between good and evil. Ntsikana was a man of peace and submission, and his cosmology was one of peace and submission.'[30]

Nuances aside, this observation reaches to the heart of the Xhosa dilemma: war or accommodation? Xhosa history suggests that these were not mutually exclusive options and, as seen in the response of Ntsikana, accommodationism is rarely totally devoid of resistance. Subsequent religious developments indicate furthermore that the divide between peaceful religious protest, effective political action and violent resistance is often a shifting distinction. The responses of Nxele and Ntsikana were not as fundamentally different as is often indicated.

The British had ostensibly fought the war in support of Ngqika, but as soon as it ended he was forced to surrender a further 3 000 square miles of territory as a buffer zone within which the Mfengu (Fingo), fleeing the effects of the *Mfecane*, were settled on the advice of the Methodist missionary John Ayliff. From the British side it paid off, as the Mfengu fought loyally on behalf of the colony in subsequent wars. Ngqika's comment, in turn, tells his side of the story: 'Though protected, I am rather oppressed by my protectors.'[31]

A tragic but not unrelated religious response came to mark a turning point in the frontier conflict. The War of the Axe (the seventh frontier war) ended in 1847 with the Xhosa being required to acknowledge the sovereignty of the Crown. The eighth frontier war, 'the longest and most costly in blood and treasure that the Cape Colony had ever engaged in', followed in less than two years and Xhosa independence was doomed.[32] Their political structures were fragmented, their culture had been destroyed by missionary and other colonial initiatives, and their land and cattle were depleted. Only a miracle could save them, and the young woman prophet Nongqause told of a vision requiring the killing of cattle and refusal to cultivate the lands, in response to which the ancestors would replenish their riches and drive the whites from the region. Almost half a million cattle are estimated to have been killed and thousands of Xhosa died. Devastated and reduced to starvation, 30 000 Xhosa surrendered themselves to the colonists, offering their labour in return for sustenance.

It is often suggested that desperation and religious fervour had given rise to an act of national suicide. More plausibly it can be seen as an act of national sacrifice in reaction to the hunger, oppression and alienation of a proud people, devastated by colonial exploitation and expropriation. Whatever the cause, the incident contributed significantly in providing a solution to the colonists' need for wage labour and to Sir George Grey's 'civilisation policy', designed to make the Xhosa economically and politically dependent on the colony.

Religious resistance continued well after any realistic chance of Xhosa independence had passed. It showed itself in attitudes such as that of the black Presbyterian church leader, Tiyo Soga. 'Be proud of what you are,' he told black Christians. He remained within the institutional church structure and some saw him as an accommodationist. For others he offered an important challenge to white missionary domination.[33] But religious resistance also came in the form of a more aggressive response to the missionaries. This was seen in the action of Rev. Nehemiah Tile, who broke away from the Methodist Church in 1884 in reaction to accusations that he was 'taking part in political matters [and] stirring up a feeling of hostility against the magistrates....'[34] Pioneer of the African Indigenous Church movement (or Ethiopianism, as it was called), he founded the first mass-based African movement of a truly national kind. The Revds. Moses Mangena Mokone and J. M. Dwane also broke with the Methodist Church, and Dwane later established the Order of Ethiopia in the Anglican Church. In 1896 a manifesto released by the Ethiopian leadership declared their intent:

To unite together Christians of the African race and of various denominations in the name of Jesus Christ to solemnly work towards and pray for the day when the African people shall become an African Christian nation....

To place on record ... the great wrongs inflicted upon the African by the people of Europe and America and to urge upon Christians who wish to be clear of African blood on the day of God's judgement, to make restitution....

Finally to pursue steadily and unswervingly the policy of AFRICA FOR THE AFRICANS and look for and hasten by prayer and united effort the forming of the AFRICAN CHRISTIAN NATION by God's power and in his own time and way.[35]

African nationalism was beginning to manifest itself in a variety of forms by the turn of the century, and this is dealt with in Chapter 2. For the sake of continuity, however, the popular appeal of the black separatist Wellington Movement in the 1920s is dealt with here.

Important to note is that while resistance was intensifying in the industrial areas in response to white control of the mining industry, in the rural areas of the Eastern Cape religious protest was thriving under the charismatic although eccentric leadership of Wellington Buthelezi. The black community was, by this time, clearly divided between an elite, made up of educated Christian teachers and ministers, usually referred to by the authorities as 'progressives', and those whom they judged to be 'backward'. (D. D. T. Jabavu, a leading member of the African elite, described the latter as people 'tied by the manacles of outdated custom.')[36] The Wellington Movement, popular in the latter constituency, was ready to take up the issues that affected traditional Africans most. But it also received support from a wider constituency of people, including mission-educated blacks who had rejected the ideals of colonialism in favour of a more popular political constituency. Loosely affiliated to the *Amafelandawonye* or *Amafela* (the die-hards), a popular alliance of women, peasants and indigenous church groups opposed to the 'progessives', Buthelezi was seeking a new African Christianity. Deeply involved in community resistance, he counselled his people not to pay taxes, and promised to provide his followers with 'all that the white man can give.'[37] An extreme Africanist, he insisted: 'If at my death I go to heaven and find a white man there I shall take my hat and go out at once and even if I go to hell and there come across a white man that hell won't contain me.'[38]

The *Amafela* had become an important ingredient in politics in the Herschel district by the late 1920s and the ANC, although not sharing their ideological views, sent James Thaele to build links with the movement. 'We are a progressive race,' Thaele insisted, and demanded that whites be taught that 'they are not living up to their morals'. This was clearly a different message to that of the *Amafela* speakers. The divide that was earlier established between Nxele and Ntsikana had again emerged. The focus, of course, was slightly different, the question being whether or not whites could become part of the projected new society.

A final example of religious resistance must suffice. It concerns the activities of the prophet Enoch Mgijima and his followers, the 'Israelites', who refused to leave the village of Ntabelanga near Bulhoek in response to a government decree. This resulted in the Bulhoek massacre on 24 May 1921. Whites regarded the settlement as harbouring vagrants and stock thieves who refused to work or pay taxes. The Israelites saw it as an escape from the harsh impositions of white rule, and Mgijima told of a vision in which it was made known to him that the end of the world was approaching. He insisted that his followers remain in Ntabelanga in preparation for that event. The land, he said, had been given to them by God and no government law could deprive them of it.[39]

The Israelites went about their religious practices, but eventually police entered the village and confrontation followed as the police opened fire on 500 Israelites. Initially refusing to defend themselves, the Israelites eventually armed themselves with sticks and assegais to defend the settlement. In all, 183 Israelites were killed, approximately 100 wounded and 150 arrested. One policeman suffered a stab wound.

The Bulhoek massacre marks the beginning of a turning point in resistance politics. Slowly the Thaele recommendation of teaching the whites to live up to their own morals was no longer being viewed as a viable option. More than forty years later Nelson Mandela would look back on that event saying: 'Almost every African household in South Africa knows about the massacre of our people at Bulhoek in Queenstown district where detachments of the army and police, armed with artillery, machine guns and rifles opened fire on unarmed Africans.'[40]

As in the case of Nxele and Ntsikana, the objectives and the responses of those who opted for violent confrontation and those who resorted to a non-violent response were not vastly different. And both have been crushed consistently in a similar manner.

Rural struggles

As black resistance in South Africa has often had a religious dimension, so in rural areas people have almost invariably been drawn into this larger struggle in response to local and seemingly mundane issues – cattle diseases, land tenure, squatting, taxes, labour issues, and land ownership.

For Africans land meant survival, and their cattle were not only a source of meat and milk, but also a resource of enormous social and cultural significance. The loss of land and cattle meant the loss of political identity and social cohesion. It was here, suggests De Kiewiet, that an 'unintentional collusion' developed between the humanitarian desires of the missionaries and the selfish, exploitative motives of others in the Eastern Cape.[41] Dispossessed black people meant a cheap supply of labour for settler farmers; for the colonial powers this dispossession meant the systematic destruction of rival political powers; for the missionaries it meant the opportunity to incorporate such people into mission stations. A series of hut, poll and labour taxes was introduced with varying degrees of support from each of these constituencies, requiring blacks to sell their labour in order to pay their taxes in cash. The outcome was a once land-rich and cattle-rearing Xhosa nation reduced to dependency on white land-owners, and a migratory labour system which compelled them to sell their labour on the mines.

Missionary involvement in this process is discussed elsewhere.[42]

It is enough to note that blacks living on mission farms were usually more disadvantaged than those working for white farmers. 'Besides taxes to the state, tithes were usually required for church buildings, educational facilities, ploughs, new seed, symmetrically constructed villages and European clothes.'[43] The encounter between the Pedi and the Berlin Mission Society in the 1870s, in turn, shows that Dinkwanyane (younger brother of the Pedi paramount chief Sekhukhune) removed his people from the Botshabelo Mission precisely because free labour, a grain tithe and movement control placed them at a disadvantage in relation to the Pedi farmers who were not on mission farms. 'Where is it written down', asked Dinkwanyane, 'that the congregation must live on the land of their spiritual leader?'[44]

The early resistance of black peasant farmers to the exploitation of colonial authorities and missionaries was limited and often failed to engage people beyond a localised area. The campaigns that emerged were often of a secret or semi-covert kind, with limited and short-term goals. It was, however, this limited protest that generated a spirit of militancy which accounted for the ready response in rural areas to the political organisations that later emerged in response to the 1913 Land Act. Sol Plaatje's documentation of the effects on black tenants and squatters of this legislation in the Orange Free State provides a vivid picture of distress and anger, readily reaped by the ANC, the ICU and the South African Communist Party.[45]

Rural and local resistance on occasions led directly to events of major national significance. This is seen most clearly in Zulu resistance that endured well beyond the destruction of Dingane's army in the fateful Battle of Blood River in 1838. Despite their victory in this battle, the Boers were never able to conquer Zululand itself, and when the British took over Natal in 1843 they too were initially obliged to be content with the area south of the Tugela River.

Determined, however, to control the entire area and eager to incorporate the less than cooperative Zulu into the labour-intensive colonial economy, a British military force under Lord Chelmsford entered Zululand on 11 January 1879. Eleven days later it was routed in battle at Isandlwana, but later the same year the British defeated the Zulu in the more decisive battle of Ulundi. 'The House of Shaka', the British reported, 'would never rise again.' The question posed by Bishop John Colenso has already been noted:

But was it a *political success* [he asked], or any more than a bloody but barren victory? … The burning of Ulundi and other kraals means nothing in Zulu eyes, as I hear from natives. And there is no clear evidence as yet that the loss of so many warriors … has broken the spirit of the natives.[46]

In the tried and tested policy of divide and rule, Zulu was pitted against Zulu, and when Cetshwayo was allowed to return to the territory in 1884 after spending four years in exile, he was obliged to rely on British support to help him counter the rival chief Zibhebhu, who had gained influence under the British policy of placing the territory under the jurisdiction of rival chiefs. Cetshwayo died a year later and was replaced by Dinuzulu, who defeated Zibhebhu, but in 1887 Zululand was annexed to the British Empire.

In this milieu it was a broad-based rural reaction that enabled Dinuzulu to engage in a campaign of resistance that led to his arrest and banishment to St Helena in 1889. When he returned in 1898 most of the best land was firmly in the grip of white settlers and Zululand had been formally incorporated into Natal. His return nevertheless rekindled Zulu loyalties, culminating in a series of rural revolts including the Bambatha rebellion in 1906 (discussed later). Imprisoned for high treason in 1908, he was exiled to the Transvaal two years later.

When the British took possession of Natal in 1843, they declared a policy of 'benevolent' rule.[47] Native Affairs Secretary, Sir Theophilus Shepstone, who projected himself as 'father and protector' of the 'natives', won the favour of most missionaries who were convinced that the defeat of the Zulu kingdom was a prerequisite for the success of the gospel and civilisation among the Zulu people. Bishop John Colenso, a supporter of Zulu independence and culture, stood out almost alone among the missionaries in seeing through Shepstone's designs.[48]

Wars of occupation were fought throughout the country and resistance struggles resulted in the mobilisation of black people in all districts. Reference has already been made to the wars between colonists and Xhosa in the Eastern Cape, and to the border conflicts in the Orange River area. The British subdued the Zulu in Natal, and in the Transvaal and the Orange Free State the Boers subjugated the indigenous populations wherever they trekked. Basutoland (Lesotho) survived largely on account of the leadership of Moshoeshoe, who played off Boer and Brit against each other, insisting that whites in the area were 'mere passers-by'. Yet finally he was obliged to agree to annexation by the British to prevent the whole of his territory from being carved up into Boer farms. Swaziland, in turn, became a Transvaal Crown Colony after the Anglo–Boer War in 1902. Sekhukhune's Pedi withstood the on-slaught of the white hunger for land longer than any chiefdom in the northern territories, but they too eventually capitulated in response to combined British, Boer and Swazi forces in 1879.

The changed character of resistance after the defeat of the African chiefs in war has already been referred to in the Introduc-tion. It included strikes, labour boycotts, desertions among inden-tured labour on Boer farms, murder and rebellion, as well as the beginning of organised political work among the dispossessed.

Beinart and Bundy's research into anti-dipping movements pro-vides a helpful insight into the kind of localised rural acts of resistance which occurred in various parts of the country after the wars of resistance and the eventual loss of independence.[49] It illus-trates how, within a seemingly apolitical climate of resentment and discontent, rural developments which in a different atmosphere would be regarded as 'progressive' became foci for rebellion.

When Lieutenant-Colonel Hartigan arrived with his troops in East Griqualand in November 1914, Kokstad (the administrative centre) was 'full of refugees from farms and trading stores from several neighbouring districts, its court-house was pressed into emergency use as a fort and there were barbed wire entanglements everywhere'.[50] The local male population had been armed and in Mount Fletcher the magistrate had issued rifles (but no ammuni-tion!) to 'loyal Bhacas'. The occasion was the gathering of an estimated 1 600 'anti-dipping dissidents', armed with assegais and rifles.

The dipping of cattle had become enmeshed with other issues, and was only one of the grievances around which popular resent-ment to the colonial administration had crystallised. Dipping-tanks and sheds had become symbols of white interference. Some dips were burned and dynamited. Others were boycotted. Women sta-tioned themselves at other dipping tanks, driving the cattle away, and those who operated the dips were threatened and physically assaulted.

East Coast fever was a tick-borne cattle disease that could be controlled only through the regular dipping of all cattle. The problem was that this became a costly exercise administered through the resented Glen Grey council system, and financed by an annual tax and a halfpenny-per-head dipping charge. It was, however, essentially the political dimension, involving what was perceived to be the most far-reaching intervention into the affairs of the local populace since annexation in 1875, that did most to fuel the fires of discontent.

The response began with non-violent protests, and, despite threats, never evolved into armed confrontation. 'We shall be pleased to be prosecuted,' groups of peasant farmers informed the authorities. Public meetings were held, but when these met with no success the responses became more radical. An added dimension of 'sedition' emerged when it was rumoured that German missionaries were informing people that, if the Germans were able to withstand the attack by South African troops on German South West Africa, they (together with Boer rebels resisting the decision of the Louis Botha government to go to war on the side of Britain) would put an end to dipping and abolish colonial rule! Most British missionaries, in turn (failing to show an understanding for the complex political issues involved), simply argued that it was to the advantage of the populace to dip their cattle. Hartigan's troops were ultimately content to 'police' the conflict, but the message of those who supported the resistance was clear: 'Don't pay your taxes.' 'Don't attend mission schools.' 'Don't dip your cattle.'[51]

Polarisation between the subjected and the subjector was such that virtually all issues, almost in spite of the cost, could be politicised in quest of a goal well beyond the confines of the immediate objective. This becomes clear in the controversy surrounding education.

Resistance in education

Political organisation around local and specific issues is nowhere more clearly seen than in the resistance that occurred in relation to mission school education.

For a significant group of people, mission education became a symbol of oppression in much the same way as cattle-dipping had become in East Griqualand. Despite the obvious benefits of mission education, there is evidence to support the case of those who condemned it as an arm of political imperialism.

The first schools were introduced in the Cape in 1658 to teach slaves the language, culture and religion of their masters – but the slaves ran away despite the promise of a glass of brandy and two inches of tobacco as a reward for completing their lessons![52] Not to be deterred, almost two hundred years later, in 1834 the authorities recognised the need for still more schools with the purpose of instilling 'social discipline' into the now emancipated slaves. Sir George Grey, British governor of the Cape in the 1850s, identified mission schools as the key to making blacks 'useful servants, consumers of our goods [and] contributors to our revenue', and the Natal Native Commission meeting in 1881 agreed that teaching Africans 'to read and write, without teaching them to work, is not doing them any good'.[53]

The distinction between those regarded by colonial officials as 'progressive' and those dismissed as 'backward' was made almost directly in relation to mission education. Certainly groups such as the *Amafela* in the Herschel district saw mission education as elitist and as undermining effective mass resistance. At least prior to the Education Act of 1865, which imposed 'manual labour' on school curricula, in mission schools like Healdtown, Lovedale and Zonnebloem the curriculum was based on Latin, Greek, English, other European languages, science and mathematics. Zonnebloem was, in fact, deliberately established in 1858 to provide an education for the 'sons of chiefs' as a means of equipping them to be enlightened (and anglicised) leaders of the future.[54]

Even after the introduction of the 1865 Education Act, 'school people' continued to constitute a class separated from the organic struggle of blacks. They frequently condemned the leaders of the black separatist churches and *Amafela* groups as politically irresponsible, and often rejected popular political initiatives, such as the anti-dipping campaign and work stoppages, as counter-productive.

In 1877 Dr Langham Dale, the Superintendent General of Education, was able to observe that the 'kid-glove era' of black education had come to an end, and that 'saw, plane, hammer and spade had taken its place'.[55] But it was precisely this shift which made mission education such a contentious issue among 'school people' and students as well as those traditionally opposed to its elitism. D. D. T. Jabavu, professor at the South African Native College at Fort Hare, gave expression to the now broader opposition to mission education in protesting that 'manual labour' consisted of 'sweeping yards, repairing roads, cracking stones and so on, and it is done by boys … as task work enforced by a time-keeper, and under the threat of punishment'.[56] Women students were, in turn, subjected to their own kind of social conditioning, being trained in cooking, baking, sewing, ironing and tailoring to equip them to be housewives and domestic workers.[57]

The educational quality of schools differed, as did the ideological commitments of teachers. Despite the consequence of inculcating colonial ideals into students, mission schools also produced some of southern Africa's most significant black leaders. The fear nevertheless existed that the provisions of the 1865 Education Act were intended to train students for a menial station in life. The wrath of 'progressive' and 'backward' Africans alike was provoked, and as the nineteenth century drew to a close the opposition to mission education intensified around student resistance to mission discipline and authoritarianism. The first recorded large-scale student rebellion erupted at Lovedale in 1873, but, in the decades that followed, institutions that recorded significant student unrest included Healdtown and Clarkebury in the Eastern Cape, Adams College in Natal, and Kilnerton in the Transvaal.[58]

The repertoire of student action – physical damage to school property, arson, class boycotts, and attacks on teachers – emerged in response to specific issues such as school and hostel accommodation, food, school discipline and the quality of teaching.[59] Yet, as was the case with the anti-dipping campaign, these specific issues usually reflected broader *political* discontent. Hyslop's analysis of student unrest, for example, shows that the 'authoritarian power relations of the missions' were seen by students as reflecting those of the wider society.[60]

Student protest did not, however, rise and ebb only in response to the level of political crisis in the wider community. It also fuelled the wider crisis. As the questioning of the role of missionaries in colonial and post-colonial society intensified, so mission schools became an ideologically contested terrain (anticipating the post-1976 education crisis in black schools). This had serious implications for the wider community. Whether the immediate issue being contested was food, discipline or textbooks, the real issue was power and resistance to externally imposed decision-making and authority. It is enough to recognise that the most localised manifestations of discontent and agitation were symptoms of a wider culture of resistance that penetrated every aspect of colonial society.

Women's resistance

There are few references to the role of women in the resistance struggles of the nineteenth century, which is perhaps the most telling statement that can be made on the status of black women. Trapped in obscurity by the ideology of racial 'inferiority' ingrained and maintained by colonists, by sexual discrimination and male domination embedded in the traditions of both African and Western societies, and by the exploitation inherent in the emerging industrialisation process, black women have borne the brunt of the devastating effects of colonial oppression.[61] They cannot but be viewed as the 'most oppressed of the oppressed' in the South African resistance struggle.[62]

Often forming the nuclei of protest and resistance groups, women have always constituted the majority in both the indigenous and established churches in South Africa. Women's unions imposed their character on rural life, with reports of the Methodist *manyano* in their distinctive scarlet uniforms 'making the whole world seem red with their jackets'.[63] Drawn into alliances with broader groups like the *Amafela*, which drew them into political altercations, the women were also in conflict with the leadership of their own churches, who shunned political controversy. Women with a base in the church and other community structures were prominent in a variety of rural protests, from trading-store boycotts to the anti-dipping campaign and the right to brew beer. They instinctively realised that meaningful change in their status was not only tied up with the destruction of colonialism (and eventually apartheid) but needed the institution of a radically different kind of new society.

This particular feminist thrust to the South African resistance struggle has not always been positively affirmed and only in more recent times has it emerged as a major issue on the liberation agenda. The historical reality of the exploitation of both black women and black men has, however, grounded the concerns of women in the fight against political and economic structures. This has given rise to a feminist movement which has refused to separate the issues of individual identity that dominate bourgeois forms of feminism in the First World from the broader economic and political ingredients of struggle.

It was the 1913 campaign against carrying passes in the Orange Free State that thrust women into national political prominence.[64] Sol Plaatje wrote of the events at the time:

After exhausting all constitutional means on behalf of their women ... the male natives of the municipalities of the Province of the Orange 'Free' State saw their women folk throwing off their shawls and taking the 'law' into their own hands. A crowd of 600 women, in July 1913, marched on the municipal offices and asked to see the mayor....[65]

The record of the African People's Organisation states:

On that day, the native women declared their womanhood. Six hundred daughters of South Africa taught the arrogant whites a lesson that will never be forgotten. Headed by the bravest of them, they marched to the magistrate, hustled the police out of their way and kept shouting and cheering until His Worship emerged from his office and addressed them, thence they proceeded to the Town Hall. The women had now assumed a threatening attitude. The police endeavoured to keep them off the steps … the gathering got out of control. Sticks could be seen flourishing overhead and some came down with no gentle thwacks across the skulls of the police, who were bold enough to stem the onrush. 'We have done with pleading, we now demand,' shouted the women.[66]

The anti-pass campaign spread to other Free State dorps: Jagersfontein, Winburg, Kroonstad and Senekal. Many of the women forfeited the option of a fine 'as a means of bringing their grievances before the notice of the public', and 'soon there were reports of gaols being too full to handle all the prisoners'.[67]

By the end of the year the Bantu Women's League was formed, with Charlotte Maxeke as its first president. A new era had dawned.

The Bambatha rebellion

It was the Bambatha rebellion in 1906 (the last time that Africans would resort to organised armed rebellion for more than fifty years) which heralded the close of this early period of resistance. The next time armed struggle would be considered as a serious option would be in the 1960s with the emergence of *Umkhonto we Sizwe* and *Poqo*, the armed wings of the African National Congress (ANC) and the Pan-Africanist Congress (PAC) respectively.

Natal was a troubled area at the turn of the century, and tensions came to a head with the introduction of a poll tax in 1906. This led to a series of confrontations between the authorities and the people who refused to pay the tax, well-illustrated in the confrontation with Bambatha, chief of the small Zondi clan in the Greytown area.

At first hesitant to side with those who refused to pay the tax, Bambatha found himself increasingly drawn to support them. Politically astute, he claimed the support of Dinuzulu, the last of the significant nineteenth-century chiefs, thus showing his awareness of the loyalty which the name of the Zulu king evoked among embittered peasants.[68]

Hunted by the colonial authorities, Bambatha took refuge with his followers among the Chube under their 96-year-old chief Sigananda in the Nkandla Forest. On 10 June 500 warriors were massacred by colonial troops, Sigananda was arrested and Bambatha killed. His head was displayed throughout the countryside as a gruesome warning to other would-be rebels. Rebellion, however, soon spread to other areas; the most significant uprisings erupted in Mapumulo, but these too were crushed. Some 3 000 Africans and approximately 30 whites died in the fighting.

A new age of resistance was in the process of being born. It would transcend tribal differences, and resistance fighters would for generations refuse to carry weapons. It would be more enduring and better coordinated, although initially moderate, cautious and compromising. The declaration of Union in 1910 on the basis of white electoral control and the 1913 Land Act shattered the illusions of Africans who thought their absorption into white society was a formality, and a number of important black political organisations began to emerge. A broad-based nationalist struggle was developing which came to a head with the banning of the ANC and PAC in 1960 – a watershed that again raised the question as to whether armed struggle was the only viable means of struggle still available against a regime that outlawed all serious political alternatives. It was also the beginning of a time of intense conflict in the church, which would eventually be compelled seriously to consider questions of resistance, violence and liberation – issues which the dominant church had hitherto chosen simply to ignore.

2
Modern resistance

Modern resistance was born with the discovery of diamonds in 1867 and the Witwatersrand goldfields in 1886. The resultant demand for a cheap and regular supply of labour transformed both the demography and the political economy of the region, and saw the birth of a national resistance struggle that continues today to challenge the authority and legitimacy of the South African regime.

Migrant labour was not a new phenomenon in the region when black workers began to flock to the mines. The Khoisan had been almost totally dependent on frontier farmers in the Eastern Cape since the latter part of the eighteenth century, and since the 1857 cattle-killing the Xhosa had roamed from farm to farm in the colony in search of work. The Pedi had been making the long trek to work on farms in the Cape Colony since the 1850s, hoping to earn enough money to buy guns with which to defend their land against Boer encroachment, and the Sotho had long been working on farms in the Orange Free State. But the discovery of minerals was to establish the practice of exploitative and migratory labour on a qualitatively different scale. Within five years of the discovery of the first diamond, 50 000 migrant Africans were flocking to the diamond fields in Kimberley each year. The development of the gold industry on the Witwatersrand had even greater consequences, being a cause of the Anglo–Boer War and thrusting into political servitude and economic dependency the black population of the entire southern African region, which produced a manifestation of black resistance on a national scale not hitherto seen in South Africa.

An efficiency the Boers could never muster
When the Peace of Vereeniging brought the Anglo–Boer War to an end in May 1902, the document of surrender ensured that blacks would not be given the vote in the former republics before the restoration of

self-government. Although this was often seen as a political victory for the Boers, the imperial rulers knew that it was also in their interests and those of the English-dominated mining industry not to allow blacks to progress beyond a certain station in life. When the Act of Union therefore brought the two defeated Boer republics and the British colonies under one flag in 1910, the hopes of the African elite of being incorporated into 'white' society were shattered. The constitution of the newly-established Union of South Africa institutionalised racial and economic discriminations and laid the foundations for a long and protracted political struggle.

The burning intent behind British imperialist ideas had long been the incorporation of all the African chiefdoms, independent Boer republics and separate British colonies under the umbrella of British economic interest. In less than 25 years Griqualand East and West, Sehukhune's Pedi, Bechuanaland, Zululand, Lobengula's Ndebele, Pondoland, the Orange Free State and South African Republic, and Swaziland all came under British rule.

Coercive legislation had long been used in the Cape and elsewhere to ensure a regular supply of labour. The Masters and Servants laws, for example, which governed the employment contract system, dated back to 1856. But it was the Glen Grey Act, enacted by the Cape parliament in 1894, that set the scene for what was to come. In the words of mine-owner and Cape politician Cecil Rhodes, 'it removed natives from a life of sloth and laziness, teaching them the dignity of labour, made them contribute to the prosperity of the state, and made them give some return for our wise and good government'.[1]

The Glen Grey Act reduced the size of plots allocated to Africans, forcing them to seek work on white-owned farms and, more particularly, in the mining industry. A ten-shilling labour tax was imposed on all black males who did not accept a contract to work on the mines for at least three months a year. To this was added a hut tax, eventually replaced with a head tax to provide a wider tax base and compel more males to work on white farms and in the mining industry. A poll tax, which had to be paid in cash, was in addition imposed on all sixteen-year-old males (despite the fact that they had no vote), ensuring the availability of still more black labour.[2] The Bambatha rebellion, discussed in the previous chapter, was a direct consequence of this legislation.

Such legislation was not, however, sufficient in itself to meet the growing labour demands of the mining industry. The Chamber of

Mines therefore formed the Rand Native Labour Association in 1896 as a means of recruiting labour, with an agreement between mines not to compete with each other in doing so. Acting on behalf of mine-owners, the Association warned: 'At present there is no guarantee that tomorrow the Rand will not be boyless. That must be remedied in the interest of the capitalist: there should be some system under which the supply is certain and cannot fail.'[3]

The post-war British administration of Lord Alfred Milner, whose task it was to create the proposed 'system', rose to the challenge and introduced a more sophisticated system of control over African workers than ever before.[4] Pass laws were more strictly imposed, legal procedures were developed to deal with breach of contract, a register of finger-prints was introduced, a non-competitive mechanism of hiring black labour was refined, and a new understanding between the mine-owners and the state began to emerge. Legal restraints on the bargaining power and individual rights of Africans were, in the words of Thomas Pakenham, 'now to be applied with an efficiency that the Boers had never been able to muster'.[5] When the first Union government took office under General Louis Botha in 1910, the ground had been prepared for an alliance of Afrikaner and English whites against the black majority and for a coalition of classes which would in time include workers as well as industrial, mining and landed capitalists. The economic foundation had also been laid for a future apartheid system. The coalition, however, was one that would immediately have to deal with its own internal class-contradictions as well as the growing discontent of a black population which was politically and constitutionally excluded from the union.

It was essentially the Land Act, passed in 1913, that legalised the long process of land dispossession reaching back to the earliest days of colonisation. Revised in 1936, it ensured that 86,3 per cent of the most fertile and mineral-rich land in South Africa belonged to whites and the remaining 13,7 per cent to blacks. More effectively and on a wider scale than the Glen Grey Act, 'it had the twin effect of suppressing the emerging African peasantry, which was proving an effective counter-class to the white farmer, and creating a pool of cheap labour in the reserves'.[6]

The church was ill-equipped to face the task which lay before it. In the face of the Boer defeat the Afrikaner churches were resolute in their concern to promote Afrikaner interests. Some English clergy had sought to act as the conscience of the British during the war, but few did not support the imperial cause. Missionaries had left their mission stations to become chaplains to the British army, and actively promoted the myth that the war was being waged on behalf of the black population.[7] After the war they, in turn, supported post-war colonial attempts to secure black labour for the mines, regarding such initiatives as part of the 'civilising' task of the church.[8] When the General Missionary Council met in 1904, its concern was with 'heathenism' and 'Romanism' rather than the violation of black rights. It met again two years later, but despite the acceptance of a resolution to 'watch over the interests of native races, and where necessary to influence legislation on their behalf', little changed.[9] The growth of the African Indigenous Churches, already referred to in Chapter 1, was a direct response to the indifference of the institutional churches to black political concerns as well as a religious manifestation of the African nationalism which prevailed at the time.[10]

A mood of alarm and unrest

While blacks were driven to the mines to seek employment, whites flocked in the same direction; but at first their dreams of job security and material gain seemed unlikely to materialise. 'Privileges were not handed to the white working class on a platter; they had to fight for these every inch of the way.'[10] White miners' strikes erupted in 1907, 1913, 1914 and again in 1922.

White labour held a revolver to the head of capital, the state and the capitalist world system, and gave its message: You may have incorporated blacks as super-exploitable workers in a super-exploitative system, but you're going to have to make a deal with us. We're going to force you to, because we can.[12]

The 1922 Rand Revolt was decisive in this regard, emerging as a watershed in white politics. It united English and Afrikaner workers against what they perceived as economic and political collusion between mining magnates and the government of General J. C. Smuts. The workers sang the 'Red Flag' and marched beneath a banner with the distorted slogan, 'Workers of the world fight and unite for a white South Africa!'[13]

Cannons roared in the streets of Johannesburg; Lewis guns spat from aeroplanes; soldiers and special police charged against barricaded strikers. The end of bloody fighting was the end of the strike. The demands of the mining companies prevailed.[14]

Within two years the long premiership of Smuts had ended and the Pact government of Col. Frederic Creswell's Labour Party and General J. B. M. Hertzog's National Party was in power. One consequence was a white labour aristocracy. Despite periodic tensions and even serious conflict between white workers and management, both would learn what could be gained by maintaining an alliance against black labour.

An equally important alliance was, in the meantime, slowly emerging to bridge the rift between the African mission-educated elite (situated largely in the Cape and Natal), the peasantry and the black proletariat on the goldfields.

The educated black leadership, who had formerly looked to less volatile options for redressing the situation, were slowly coming to recognise strikes by black miners and resistance by agricultural workers as the only effective avenue of political opposition. A direct consequence of this shift was the mushrooming of political organisations that incorporated blacks into a new-found alliance.

Organisations

During the nineteenth century African nationalism had found expression regionally, essentially on a tribal basis, and primarily in response to specific local points of grievance as identified in Chapter 1; issues such as cattle-dipping, educational crises and the collection of taxes. This process would continue, but a new dimension of national organised resistance was beginning to emerge as the focus of black response to the declaration of Union in 1910 and the Land Act of 1913. The response of the churches to these developments (as the foundation stones of white supremacy and black dispossession) was ambiguous. They regarded the land allocation as too restrictive and disruptive of black family life, but failed to concern themselves with the fundamental ideological intent of the legislation. If hitherto there had been some evidence of blacks (if only the mission-educated elite) seeing the churches as a channel for communicating their views, there was now evidence of disillusionment. A brief chronology of the birth of national organisations identifies the scope of the new national awakening among black people.

— The first indication of a black nationally coordinated organisation came in 1898 with the establishment of the *South African Native Congress* (SANC). It was scarcely an effective national body, but one of its branches, the Orange River Colony Native Congress,

called the South African Native Council into session in Bloemfontein in 1909 in response to the all-white National Convention held
in October 1908, which supported a constitution for the Union of
South Africa (to be established in 1910) that effectively excluded
blacks from the political process. In 1912 came the emergence of
the *South African Native National Congress* (SANNC), later to be
known as the *African National Congress* (ANC), and the stage was set
for a more effective form of African resistance on a national scale
– although still restrained and moderate. SANNC was concerned
with little more than the serious implementation of Cecil Rhodes's
dictum, 'equal rights for all civilised men from the Cape to the
Zambezi'.[15] With no intention of assuming power, the original
movement has been described by Fatima Meer as essentially 'a club
of chiefs and intellectuals'.[16]

— The 'coloured' people (descendants of the Khoisan, slaves,
the Griquas and racially mixed couples) were also slowly beginning
to throw off a sense of political dependency. The *African Political*
(later *People's) Organisation* (APO) was established in 1902, initially
with its own set of racial prejudices. An early leader, Abdullah
Abdurahman, insisted, for example, that 'the educated class of
coloured people in Cape Town could no longer be treated as part
of an undifferentiated mass of uneducated barbarians'.[17] But as
national events developed in response to the 1910 constitution, the
APO was transformed into a national organisation committed to
non-racial politics.

— The *Bantu Women's League* emerged a year later, in 1913. As
already noted (in Chapter 1), this was in response to the Land Act
passed that same year and the imposition of the pass law on African
women in the Orange Free State. Although the League lost the
organisational initiative among women in the 1920s, it was the only
women's group invited to the important All-African Convention in
1935.[17] It was also the early successes of the Bantu Women's League
which established a momentum among women that would again
flourish with the women's march on the Union Buildings in Pretoria at the height of the defiance campaign in the 1950s.

— The *Industrial and Commercial Workers' Union* (ICU) was formed
in 1919, partly owing to the reluctance and organisational inability
of the ANC to involve itself in the strike activities of black workers.
It 'grew into a massive force in a very short period of time.... Hardly
a town or a *dorp* but had its ICU branch.'[19] Despite continuous police
harassment, internal divisions, and the eventual alienation of the

leaders from members, which led to the collapse of the ICU in 1928, it gave rise to a tradition of labour union engagement in broader political issues that would become an important and enduring characteristic of the resistance struggle. Despite the later failures of leadership, ICU was the most significant black resistance organisation in the early part of the twentieth century.[20]

— The *Communist Party of South Africa* (CPSA) was founded two years after the ICU in 1921, adopting in 1928 a plan for 'an independent native republic as a stage towards a workers' and peasants' republic'. It was a policy that not all Communists supported. Party leader Sydney Bunting, for example, feared it would alienate white workers and drive them towards Afrikaner nationalism. James la Guma, secretary of the ANC in Cape Town, suggested, on the other hand, that white workers were 'saturated with imperialist ideology' and could not be trusted. And yet, as a means towards a greater goal, the CPSA joined forces with white workers on issues such as the 1922 Rand mineworkers' revolt.[21]

— The *South African Indian Congress* (SAIC) was formed in 1923, with the *Natal Indian Congress* already having been founded in 1894. Indians first arrived in Natal as indentured workers in response to a labour crisis on the sugar plantations, and traders and merchants followed in their wake, as did Mohandas Gandhi (in 1893), who soon emerged as the key political leader in the Indian community. He mobilised the Indian community through his *Satyagraha* movement against the decision of the post-war Transvaal administration to require Indians to be finger-printed and registered as part of a policy of segregation, but showed no interest in the violation of African rights. Eventually, under pressure from Smuts, he agreed to support registration in return for which (according to Gandhi) Smuts had agreed to repeal the Act. Smuts denied having agreed to this undertaking and Gandhi's support base collapsed. He continued to pursue his campaigns of resistance in Natal and the Transvaal and eventually returned to India in 1914. The SAIC was formed in 1923 to 'oppose the growing segregationalist tendencies in local and national legislation', and later entered into a pact with the ANC.[22]

Within little more than twenty years of the declaration of Union the black population was grouped into organisations that would in the years ahead be drawn ever closer together. In the meantime black workers had resorted to the only viable means of resistance available to them – strikes.

Strikes

Black workers resisted the effects of proletarianisation from the beginning. New urban blacks carried with them into the cities the religious and cultural values that had developed through their encounters with missionaries in the previous century. Some reacted against this heritage, for some religion became a political opiate, and others adapted it to cope with the new forms of exploitation they experienced. A Xhosa teacher, Enoch Sontonga, for example, composed the hymn *Nkosi Sikelel' iAfrika* (God Bless Africa) in Johannesburg's Nancefield hostel in 1897, giving religious expression to the suffering of blacks and the longing for deliverance. In 1925 it would be adopted as the anthem of the ANC.[23]

The institutional churches essentially remained aloof from this resistance culture. Their concern was with saving souls and the moral behaviour of the workers, promoting a middle-class character alien to both black and white miners. 'The sons of toil are mainly conspicuous by their absence from church services,' lamented a 1911 edition of the *Methodist Churchman*.[24] At the same time industry needed labour and the churches worked in cooperation with recruitment agencies and sought to provide the kind of 'manual education' through mission schools best suited to equip blacks for the labour market.[25] Cochrane, for example, shows evidence of this collaboration, citing a substantial donation made by the Witwatersrand Native Labour Association to the mission work of the church.[26]

The resistance which came from black workers who, like their white counterparts, began to flex their muscles early in the history of the mining industry was in direct contradiction to the teaching of the institutional churches. The first organised forms of black labour unrest occurred in the gold mines in 1901–2 and the diamond mines in 1907, while in 1913 (following the success of a white workers' strike) black workers on a number of mines engaged in sustained strikes against 'the colour bar which blocks practically all opportunities of promotion'.[27] Strikes continued in the years that followed and 1920 saw the largest and most effective industrial action of this period when more than 70 000 black workers went out on strike. They were driven back to work at the point of bayonets, while white workers ignored the plea of black workers for solidarity. The rift between black and white workers was growing ever wider.

The 1922 Rand Revolt had made mine-owners and government

alike wary of provoking the white unions,[28] but the reservoir of black unskilled labour which industry and government had generated seemed endless, making the black proletariat a sustained target of exploitation. Hertzog, despite his clear and uncompromising white supremacist stance, courted and received the support of CPSA, APO and ICU leadership, who saw his anti-imperialist and pro-worker policy as eventually being to the benefit of all workers.[29] He was elected to power with Creswell in the 1924 Pact government and immediately turned his back on these black organisations to promote the cause of the white workers.

Firing the souls of the masses

Unskilled and semi-skilled white work-seekers (most of whom were devoutly religious Afrikaners who had recently arrived in the cities from the rural areas) were living side by side with blacks in urban slums in dire poverty when the Pact government came to power. But whites had the vote, and essentially the vote of these workers brought the government to power. 'An unholy alliance', says W. A. de Klerk, was being established 'between Christian Afrikaners and British Bolsheviks.'[30]

Committed to solving the 'poor white problem', the Pact government through its 'civilised labour policy' justified an increase in the wages of whites, and thousands of black workers were declared redundant. Not prepared to support the kind of direct action demanded by black workers, through strikes, the burning of passes and the refusal to pay taxes, the ICU collapsed in 1928. But worker unrest continued.

Hertzog's concern was, however, more than the creation of a privileged white working class. Through a series of 'Hertzog bills' he sought also to curtail even the limited participation by blacks in government that already existed. Initially unable to get the necessary parliamentary support for this legislation, he reintroduced the bills in 1935 with support from the newly-formed United Party led by himself and Smuts. The most important features of the bills were the prohibition on blacks owning land outside the 'Native Reserves' and the removal of Africans in the Cape (the only area where they had a restricted franchise) from the voters' roll.

News of the bills unleashed the biggest show of black resistance to date. On 16 December 1935 over 400 delegates from all major political groups in the country gathered in Bloemfontein at the All-African Convention (AAC). The secretary of the Convention,

Selby Msimang, insisted that the time had come to 'agitate' to 'fire the soul' and to engage in the 'intense organisation and persistent education of the masses along systematic and persuasive lines....'[31] It would, however, take a further decade before the shift toward mass-organised resistance would take place, and the immediate proposals in support of militant action were rejected by the conference in favour of prayer meetings, appeals, petitions and delegations to meet with government officials. All to no avail. The Hertzog bills became law on 6 April 1936. The constituent groups in the AAC, in turn, decided (against the counsel of some) to participate in the newly formed Native Representatives' Council.

Black groups, including the ANC, had consistently turned away from radical action. Early attempts by the ICU to take a tougher stance were lost in compromise and the eventual collapse of the ICU. The appeals and prayer meetings of the AAC came to naught. At the same time blacks witnessed the emergence of the *Gesuiwerde* (Purified) National Party in 1934 in protest at what was seen by some whites as the 'too moderate' stance of Hertzog. They witnessed too the inroads made by the Afrikaner Broederbond, an exclusive Afrikaner secret society that traced its origins back to 1918, and the commemorative Great Trek in 1938, which unleashed yet a further wave of white Afrikaner patriotism.

The next decisive step in white politics came with the decision of the Union parliament to enter the war on the side of Britain in 1939. Hertzog resigned as prime minister and Smuts, who became prime minister in his stead, took South Africa into war. The pro-Nazi *Ossewabrandwag* opposed the move, and its military wing, the *Stormjaers* (Stormtroopers), sabotaged government installations and broke up public gatherings in militant acts of protest. The ANC, on the other hand, supported the decision of the government to go to war against Germany, although blacks who joined the armed forces were restricted to non-combatant roles such as driving, digging trenches, carrying stretchers, cooking, cleaning and other menial tasks. The war nevertheless transformed the attitude of blacks. Colonised and oppressed people around the world, inspired by the commitment of European nations to be free in the face of the Nazi tyranny, demanded their own freedom. South Africa's oppressed majority was no exception.

Political developments inside South Africa were at the same time moving in a similar direction. The collapse of the ICU, the uncompromising stance of Hertzog, the tendency of mine-owners to favour white workers, and the economic depression had introduced a new determination into the black community.

The Congress Youth League (CYL), which included Nelson Mandela, Walter Sisulu, Oliver Tambo and Anton Lembede, was slowly gaining control of the ANC. Critical of the elitism of ANC leadership and of its 'giving way in the face of oppression', the CYL issued a manifesto at its inaugural conference in March 1944. 'The hour of youth has struck! As the forces of National Liberation gather momentum, the call to youth to close ranks in order to consolidate the national Unity Front, becomes more urgent and imperative.'[32]

The Council for Non-European Trade Unions (CNETU), which had been formed in 1938, came, in turn, to show a new awareness of the nature of black oppression, which militated against the hope of the African elite that blacks would be incorporated into mainstream society. 'Let us realise', said a delegate to the 1942 CNETU congress, 'that we are oppressed, firstly as a race and secondly as workers. If this were not the case we would not have to put up so bitter a struggle for recognition of our trade unions.'[33] By the time the war ended in 1945, the CNETU could claim the support of 119 affiliated trade unions with a combined membership of 158 000 people. In 1941 the African Mine Workers' Union (AMWU) was formed, with J. B. Marks, a member of the ANC and the Communist Party, elected as its leader in 1945. A year later, in 1946, it called its members out on strike, bringing the mines on the Witwatersrand to a halt. The police smashed resistance before the CNETU could join the strike in sympathy. The immediate goal of the strike for a minimum wage of ten shillings a day was not realised and the AMWU never recovered from its defeat. Black unions would take years to overcome government action against them. 'But', to quote Magubane, 'the sheer size of the strike and especially its ability to paralyse the key industry of the country showed for the first time the power the African proletariat could wield....'[34] Resistance organisations were being pushed in the direction of mass action, and not least of all as a result of the emergence of the powerful South African Congress of Trade Unions (SACTU) in 1955.[35]

Defiance and non-cooperation

When the National Party was elected to power in 1948 a barrage of apartheid laws was enacted. These included the Group Areas Act, the Mixed Marriages Act and the Population Registration Act, with the promise to remove 'coloureds' from the common voters' roll as had been done with Africans in 1936. Protest spread, but APO and Unity Movement 'coloureds' were divided on tactics. The SAIC was committed to work with the ANC, and liberal English-speaking whites formed the Torch Commando to protest against the violation of the constitution in removing 'coloureds' from the common roll. In the meantime, at its 1949 annual conference, the ANC adopted the CYL-backed Programme of Action.

The Joint Action Committee of the ANC and SAIC, appointed to carry out this programme, appealed to the government to repeal all 'unjust laws', and 6 April 1952 (the tercentenary of the arrival of Van Riebeeck in the Cape, an event annually celebrated by whites as the *Volksplanting* or beginning of white settlement) was observed as a National Day of Prayer and Pledge. The programme further called for strategies of 'non-cooperation and non-violence as the most suitable forms of struggle in the historical conditions of South Africa.' Seeking to ensure a disciplined campaign, the committee imposed a "code of conduct"' on those sharing in the 'defiance of all unjust laws based on non-cooperation'.[36]

Although the campaign did not reach the level of a general strike, before the state was able to crush it completely, campaigns of defiance were experienced throughout the major centres of the country and the ANC was transformed into a mass movement. Actions included labour strikes, stayaways, bus boycotts, the refusal to carry passes, the breaking of curfews, standing at 'European only' counters, entering segregated buses and railway carriages, school boycotts, non-cooperation with government-appointed functionaries and the defiance of bans on public meetings. Spontaneous religious manifestations of protest spread, and days of prayer, hymn-singing, church services and fasting were declared. ANC membership is estimated to have increased from 7 000 at the beginning of the campaign to an excess of 100 000 paid-up members by the end of the year.

Violence is always latent among an oppressed people; it holds within it the possibility of anarchy and it has frequently been exploited by criminal elements to their own ends. It was not, however, until the leaders of the defiance campaign were arrested that widespread violence and rioting erupted among the people, and social analysts tend to agree that there was no serious evidence of such behaviour being condoned or advocated by resistance leaders as a means of struggle. The ANC leadership appealed to its followers to 'be peaceful, disciplined, non-violent'. Albert Luthuli, shortly to become President of the ANC, in a widely published speech entitled 'The Road to Freedom Is Via the Cross' asked the inevitable question: 'Who will deny that thirty years of my life have been spent knocking in vain, patiently, moderately and modestly at a closed and barred door?' He called for 'a new spirit ... that revolts openly and boldly against injustice'.[37]

1953 saw the introduction of the Bantu Education Act, designed to provide an education for blacks that ensured they would have, in the words of Hendrik Verwoerd who was Minister of Native Affairs at the time, no place 'above the level of certain forms of labour'.[38] Black education was almost entirely dependent on the churches at the time and they had a unique opportunity to act boldly to disrupt Verwoerd's plans but deliberately chose not to.

The tragic mistake [said Trevor Huddleston] ... lay in the failure of the churches to act together. I am convinced that had ... they approached the Prime Minister and stated that, in conscience, they could not cooperate in the implementation of the Act, at least some major concessions would have been made.[39]

The churches were not ready for that kind of showdown with the state. The Act did, however, unleash a further wave of resistance in the community. Group Areas legislation, in turn, resulted in entire communities being forcibly moved to prescribed black areas, as happened with Sophiatown in 1955. Resistance was brushed aside as the police moved in with machine guns and batons, against which the people were powerless; Soweto rose out of the veld as a newly-prescribed black area. Again the church had the opportunity to resist, recognising that the people being removed were in many instances loyal and staunch members of the institutional churches. 'The church sleeps on,' wrote Huddleston. 'The church sleeps on – though it occasionally talks in its sleep and expects (or does it?) the government to listen.'[40]

The next important phase of resistance came with the establishment of the Congress Alliance. This consisted of the ANC, SAIC, SACPO, SACTU and the Congress of Democrats (formed to unite liberal whites in 1950), and emerged as a result of grassroots work throughout the country in preparation for the writing of the Freedom Charter.[40] On 26 June 1955, 3 000 people attended the Congress of the People in Kliptown. Others were stopped at road blocks or arrested beforehand, and while the Freedom Charter was still being debated, the entire Congress was placed under arrest. After the singing of *Nkosi Sikelel' iAfrika*, debate continued while police noted the names of those present. The Charter was later ratified by the individual organisations present.

The national unity which came about from the adoption of the Freedom Charter resulted in intensive police surveillance of activists and in December 1956 some 156 people were arrested on charges of treason. All were found 'not guilty' after a four-year trial which, in turn, led to the state enacting legislation which enabled it to suppress resistance, ban organisations and detain people without having to deal with the courts.

Throughout this period women were becoming increasingly involved in organised politics, largely as a result of the defiance campaign. Despite the early successes of the Bantu Women's League, black women had not been prominently involved in organisational politics. With the launch of the Federation of South African Women in 1954, this began to change. Jointly with the ANC Women's League, FSAW organised demonstrations against the decision that African women should carry passes. 'Pass-burning'events were organised across the country. Some 2 000 women met outside the Union Buildings to present a petition to the government in October 1955, and a year later 20 000 women travelled to the capital from all parts of the country, each carrying a petition. They stood in silence outside Prime Minister Hans Strijdom's office and sang their anthem, 'Strijdom, you have tampered with the women, you have struck a rock.'[42]

Resistance was escalating elsewhere as well. The Evaton bus boycott, for example, commanded public attention and soon boycotting spread to other centres. Most notable was the boycott sparked by an increase in the bus-fare from Alexandra township to Johannesburg. Monday, 3 January 1957 saw 15 000 people walking the fifteen kilometres to the city centre and by the end of the week 60 000 had refused to use the buses. When the ANC eventually called off the boycott, 'Africanist' factions within the ANC who had resisted the broadening of the ANC's programme of action to include other groups saw this as further evidence of compromise on its part.

The Africanists eventually broke away from the ANC in April 1959 to form the Pan-Africanist Congress (PAC), under the leadership of Robert Sobukwe. Affirming a tradition present within African resistance from the earliest days of colonialism, it sought to reassert African cultural and political independence, insisting that the liberation of blacks was to come exclusively from blacks.[43] With the ANC accused of compromising on black ideals and failing to offer an adequate programme of empowering blacks, the rift between the two organisations grew ever deeper. Committed to the ideological assumption that the masses were ready to respond spontaneously to a creative initiative, Sobukwe informed the Commissioner of Police that the PAC would engage in 'a sustained, disciplined, non-violent campaign', against the pass laws. On 21 March 1960, 20 000 people converged on Sharpeville police station in peaceful protest, ready to surrender their passes and accept arrest. Sobukwe and other leaders had been arrested at the head of a small group earlier in the day, and as the larger crowd gathered, the police opened fire and 67 people lay dead. A definite turning point in resistance had been reached.

Langa and Nyanga townships in the Western Cape erupted in protest and strike action brought Cape industry to a standstill. Things came to a head on 30 March when Philip Kgosana, a young PAC activist in Cape Town, led a march of 30 000 people along the major highway into the city. Persuaded by the chief of police to turn back in return for a promised meeting with the Minister of Justice, Kgosana was arrested when he reported for the meeting. 'Whatever the marchers may have achieved by staying in Cape Town that day,' writes Lodge, 'one thing is certain: they lost everything by going home.'[44]

'It took the police four days of continuous brutality to break the strike. They used sticks, batons, crow bars, guns and Saracen armoured cars to comb the townships and force men back to work.'[45] Altogether 1 500 people were arrested and the strike was broken. Unrest spread to other parts of the country but an era was about to close. A state of emergency was declared on 30 March, and the ANC and PAC were banned on 8 April.

The churches could not but respond. Meeting in the Cottesloe Consultation in December 1960, they concluded in a restrained response that apartheid could not be reconciled with Scripture, criticised some apartheid laws and cautiously stated there could be 'no objection in principle to the direct representation of coloured people in parliament'. As self-evident and moderate as these conclusions appeared in a broader context, for the church they constituted an important step toward direct confrontation with the state. The *Message to the People of South Africa* followed in 1968, describing apartheid as a 'pseudo-gospel' and a further fourteen years were needed for the churches to declare the theological justification of apartheid a heresy.[46] In the meantime the agenda for more radical responses by the oppressed people was being set by the repressive actions of the state.

Submit or fight

Sobukwe was in prison, Oliver Tambo had slipped out of the country to head the ANC's external office, Nelson Mandela had gone underground and other top ANC and PAC leaders were either imprisoned or driven into exile.

Since before the emergence of political organisations at the turn of the century, black leaders had consistently rejected violence as an instrument of resistance and change – and some even accepted steps towards direct non-violent action only with reluctance. Now, with their major political organisations banned, other avenues of resistance were sought.

A depleted ANC executive met secretly in June 1961 and accepted that, while its non-violent programme of action should continue, a separate organisation, *Umkhonto we Sizwe* (the Spear of the Nation), should be established to implement a campaign of carefully controlled violence. Mandela had argued that 'unless responsible leadership was given to canalise and control the feelings of people, there would be outbreaks of terrorism which would produce an intensity of bitterness and hostility between the various races of this country'.[47] The focus was the sabotage of Bantu Administration offices, post offices, electrical and railway installations. 'We hope', read a pamphlet of *Umkhonto we Sizwe*, 'that we will bring the Government and its supporters to their senses before it is too late, so that both the Government and its policies can be changed before matters reach the desperate stage of civil war.'[48]

Poqo (a Xhosa word meaning 'to stand alone') was a different kind of organisation. The leadership structure of the PAC had been virtually eliminated by state repression in 1960, and *Poqo*, consisting of isolated bands of fighters claiming allegiance to Sobukwe, emerged as the armed wing of that movement. Gail Gerhart describes *Poqo* as the manifestation of a cathartic expression of the oppressed who intuitively believed that, whatever the outcome of their violence, it had to be an improvement on the present.[49] Whatever the psychological explanation of *Poqo*, in some ways it *was* an expression of spontaneous insurrectionist impetus among sections of the oppressed.[50]

When Potlako Leballo, national secretary of the PAC, was released from prison in May 1962, he sought to coordinate the activities of *Poqo* from Basutoland but with limited success. After his release, Matthew Nkoane returned from a visit to the Eastern Cape and observed, 'I came back feeling that the PAC were going to be unable to control our chaps … the rudiments of *Poqo.*'[51] Civilians were attacked and killed while asleep, *Poqo* soldiers armed with pangas and axes advanced on white suburbs. Police action followed and this, together with internal feuds and divisions, fuelled by the promise of a general uprising and the imminent overthrow of the white regime, led to the collapse of the movement.

Umkhonto we Sizwe action coordinated from inside South Africa was seriously disrupted by a police swoop on its Rivonia headquarters in July 1963. Nelson Mandela, Govan Mbeki, Walter Sisulu, Ahmed Kathrada, Dennis Goldberg, Arthur Goldreich and others were subsequently found guilty of treason and imprisoned.

A long history of refusal to resort to revolutionary violence by the protest organisations had ended. Nelson Mandela's court testimony in 1964 illustrates the point:

They [the white regime] set the scene for violence by relying exclusively on violence to meet our people and their demands…. We have warned repeatedly that the government, by resorting continuously to violence, will breed, in this country, counter-violence amongst the people, till ultimately, the dispute between the government and my people will finish up being settled in violence and by force.

The time comes in the life of any nation when there remain only two choices – submit or fight. That time has now come to South Africa. We shall not submit and we have no choice but to hit back by all means in our power in defence of our people, our future and our freedom.[52]

The institutional church found the resort to armed revolutionary struggle almost impossible to accept, despite the fact that many of its own members were among those who would in the years ahead leave the country to train as guerilla fighters. And when the World Council of Churches eventually voted in 1970 to provide humanitarian aid to liberation armies fighting against oppressive minority regimes in southern Africa, the churches in South Africa condemned the decision.[53]

Black man, you are on your own

With the close of the Rivonia trial, the crushing of the *Poqo*

the state to this alliance, which seemed to be the only likely outcome of the fast-growing cooperation between UDF, COSATU and NUM. During this time unions that supported AZAPO were also undertaking a quest for unity and in 1986 the Azanian Confederation of Trade Unions (AZACTU) and the Council of Unions of South Africa merged – to be renamed the National Council of Trade Unions (NACTU) in April 1987. With the dream of one federation of trade unions not yet a reality, COSATU and NACTU continue to represent two different ideological emphases in the trade union movement.

The spirit of resistance had, during this time, intensified in the church as well. This was seen in the widespread support for the campaign for *Prayer for the End of Unjust Rule* on 16 June 1985, and more especially in the grassroots support for the *Kairos Document* published later that year.[65] The responses to these statements within the institutional churches varied and a longstanding latent rift within these churches between conservative and radical groups became increasingly overt.

State of emergency

School stay-aways, worker resistance, consumer boycotts, rioting, armed conflict, the military occupation of townships, murders, demonstrations and a spate of mass meetings, protest church services and other forms of protest and rebellion spread across the country. These united rural and urban people in a campaign of resistance and defiance. On 20 July 1985 a state of emergency was declared in 36 magisterial districts, and in October was extended to include the Western Cape – the first general state of emergency since 1960. Within three months 5 000 people had been detained and almost 700 killed.

After the initial declaration of the state of emergency in July, the Western Cape became a centre of unrest. The police and military fought resisters in the streets, with ambushes, dogs and tear-gas, killing both young and old. A mass march on Pollsmoor Prison was announced by Allan Boesak to demand the release of Nelson Mandela and, despite Boesak's arrest and what was described as the biggest security force presence in the city since the Kgosana march, an estimated 10 000 – 20 000 people sought to break through police barriers in an attempt to join the march. People were tear-gassed and beaten by the police, and hundreds were arrested. For two days parts of the city were under siege, and 30 people were killed and a further 300 injured.

A measure of 'control' was imposed and the state of emergency lifted but again unrest spread. The South African rand fell dramatically, Western governments began to impose limited economic sanctions against South Africa and some Western businesses withdrew from the country. Certain black townships were patrolled and cordoned off by the military, others were declared 'no-go' areas. The ANC called for the country to be made 'ungovernable', leading activists simply disappeared and others were found mysteriously murdered as right-wing informers were tried in street courts and, when found guilty, put to death. A second nation-wide state of emergency was declared on 12 June 1986.

The church restrained and in resistance

As the struggle for liberation has intensified among the oppressed people of South Africa, so the church has been increasingly drawn into this struggle – although, as already shown, its involvement has traditionally been cautious and reluctant. The churches have become deeply divided against themselves, between those who seek to apply the radical demands of the gospel for social justice, and those who seem content merely to have been on record as having condemned apartheid. It is this divide that is articulated in the *Kairos Document* and that is also theologically and socially documented in this author's *Trapped in Apartheid*.[66] The *Kairos Document* set the theological agenda for a church confronted with a liberation struggle by oppressed people. Central to this agenda are the issues of civil disobedience, armed struggle and illegitimate government, debated in the second part of this book.

Church representatives met with exiled South Africans in Lusaka in May 1987 and issued the *Lusaka Statement*. It reads in part:

We affirm the unquestionable right of the people of Namibia and South Africa to secure justice and peace through the liberation movements. While remaining committed to peaceful change, we recognise that the nature of the South African regime which wages war against its own inhabitants and neighbours compels the movements to the use of force along with other means to end oppression. We call upon the churches and the international community to seek ways to give this affirmation practical effect in the struggle for liberation in the region and to strengthen their contacts with the liberation movements.

Since adopted by the South African Council of Churches (SACC), this statement, which seeks to locate the churches on the

side of the liberation struggle, comes closer than any other statement to accepting the inevitability of armed struggle, but it does
not enjoy the support of all member churches of the SACC.[67]

History is ahead of the churches. Whatever the outcome of
ecclesial debate on the theological issues to which we now turn –
civil disobedience, revolutionary violence and state illegitimacy –
the direction and the character of the struggle is not likely to
change. Such debate may determine, however, whether the church
is to be a serious participant in that struggle or simply brushed aside
by the forces of history. It is argued in what follows that the church
has traditional resources that enable it to respond creatively to this
challenge, but a history that shows it is slow to translate this theory
into praxis.

PART TWO

Theological response

3
Civil disobedience

The preoccupation with 'law' and the affirmation of 'law and order' have been central ingredients of oppression in South Africa from the earliest days of colonialism. The dominant theological tradition of the church has, in turn, predisposed Christians to 'be subject to the governing authorities'. It is this that places the theological debate on civil disobedience at the centre of a theology of resistance.

'Law' is indeed the single most potent symbol of statecraft in the modern world. In Western mythology it denotes social order, elicits a sense of moral obligation, and cautions against the latent presence of social anarchy. This has persuaded even the boldest social reformers that in disobeying a specific law they endanger the entire legal structure of the nation. This same fear led Martin Luther King to warn in his *Letter from Birmingham City Jail,* 'In no sense do I advocate evading or defying the law…. This would lead to anarchy. One who breaks an unjust law must do it openly, lovingly … and with a willingness to accept the penalty.'[1]

Alexander M. Bickel, a former Sterling Professor of Law at Yale University, suggests that 'the zealots of the left' who put their cause before the law in resisting the Vietnam war may well have provided the prologue to Watergate. 'I don't know when Mr Nixon caught the liberals bathing, but he did walk off with their clothes…,' said Mr Bickel. Whatever we may think of this attempt to make 'law-breaking' the unique possession of the left, or the attempt to render Nixon a liberal, Bickel's understanding of the nature of law is worth noting: 'If the law itself provided that those who disagree with it for one or another ordinary reason may disregard it, the law would not be law in any significant sense, but merely another expression of opinion.'[2]

It would, however, be equally wrong to avoid the moral question by addressing only the legal question. It is never enough to justify one's actions by resorting to the defence, 'I was only obeying the law.' Such a response bears a close relationship to the appeal to 'superior orders' indulged in by successive generations of criminals who seek to escape the consequences of their deeds. The Charter of the International Military Tribunal produced by the four Allied powers at the close of World War Two as a basis for the trials of Nazi war criminals, for example, expressly provided that courts be forbidden to entertain an appeal to 'superior orders' as basis for defence.

In South Africa, until recently, the only case of reported 'superior orders' had been *Rex* v. *Smith* during the Anglo–Boer War. The court, which sat in 1900, ruled that a superior order was obligatory in all situations unless 'manifestly illegal'. Then in 1987 the Supreme Court of the Cape of Good Hope (in the *State* v. *Villet and Kruger*) found two policemen guilty despite the fact that they obeyed the command of a superior officer. Mr Justice Howie concluded that the command which resulted in the death of a young woman and the wounding of three other persons was not a lawful command. Killing of people, he ruled, was *prima facie* unlawful.[3]

If the lawfulness of an order given in the armed or police forces could not be questioned, writes Gerald Gordon QC, we would reach a state of government summed up by the satirist of autocratic Rome in the first century of this era: '*Hoc volo, sic jubeo, sit pro ratione voluntas.*' (I will have this done, so I order it done; let my will replace reasoned judgment.)[4]

If law, regardless of its intent and nature, must be obeyed simply because it is called law, we have surrendered our right to be called a reasonable, moral and democratic society. As argued in the Introduction, in a national security state where morality and democracy are no longer normative aspects of statecraft, the preservation of or quest for these values is of the utmost importance. Distorted notions of morality and democracy are also invoked by even the most undemocratic states, and these need to be undermined and rejected as part of a liberatory political process. It is this that locates civil disobedience at the centre of our quest for a world within which justice and peace are non-negotiable imperatives. Differently stated, what has also been called the *conscientious affirmation* of a moral imperative sometimes requires refusal to obey laws that may be regarded as unjust.[5] 'Civil disobedience may thus be described', writes André du Toit, 'as a kind of conscientious violation of the law which yet seeks to maintain the values that the law promotes' – or, it should be added, those values that it claims to promote.[6]

The gospel demands that where civil law contradicts the authority of God we disregard the law (Acts 4: 19), and the history of the church contains many celebrated moments of such resistance. In practice, however, it is sometimes difficult to know what is the will of God, and whether a particular law contradicts it. Different theologies and secular theories of law assess, define and understand law differently and there is no common mind within or outside the church concerning the nature or identity of an unjust or illegitimate law. Even where agreement exists, it is not easy to decide on the most effective manner in which to change or resist laws that contradict this perception of the divine will. Bluntly stated, Christian conviction about the obligation to resist unjust rule is often relativised to the point where Christians are unable to translate their moral indignation into effective political action.

Before addressing this issue of relativism, however, it is necessary to define briefly certain key terms. *Civil disobedience* is primarily a political act. It involves deliberate action designed to change laws or a political dispensation considered unaccceptable on the grounds of moral, theological or political principle. As such it differs from *conscientious objection* which is primarily an expression of moral indignation manifest in a refusal to participate in a given social or political process. Although conscientious objection often manifests itself in civil disobedience, it does not necessarily do so. Suffice it to say, in the words of Hannah Arendt, 'conscientious objection can become politically significant [only] when a number of consciences happen to coincide and the conscientious objectors decide to enter the marketplace and make their voices heard in public'.[7] Civil disobedience can also be employed as a means of political or legal reform directed against certain unjust laws, as well as a revolutionary strategy intended to bring about the collapse of a particular state on the grounds that it is illegitimate and incapable of producing just and peaceful rule.

In what follows:

1. The place of civil disobedience within five different models of law is considered, in an attempt to move beyond the confusion generated by theoretical relativism towards a viable basis for a programme of action.

2. Civil disobedience is considered as a democratic act of lawmaking which is an integral part of the ongoing democratic process,

operating at its centre. As such the notion is employed in a reformist sense.

3. Civil disobedience is considered as a means of removing what the South African Council of Churches (SACC) and several of its member churches have declared to be an illegitimate South African regime. Here civil disobedience is used in a revolutionary sense – with the term 'revolution' being employed throughout this book in the *classical* definition of 'qualitative change'.

Civil disobedience in theological and legal debate

In the models or typologies of law which follow, an attempt is made (at the level of theology and jurisprudence) to explain why some people are more ready than others to engage in civil disobedience or, theologically or morally, to condone such acts.

Law as divine obedience

The distinguishing mark of this model of law is the existence of an absolute God, a divine principle or a sacred symbol against which a legal enactment can be measured. It involves a command of God, a sacred moment in the midst of struggle, within which people are addressed in such a way that they are obliged not only to hear but to obey. The command transcends the multiplicity of human endeavours, engaging the individual or community in covenant with the sovereign God, and requiring absolute obedience whatever the cost. It engages the individual or community in a sense of vocation and calls one to be a herald and precursor of God's rule on earth.

The more bizarre distortions of this model of law are ignored in what follows. It is rather the theologically legitimate, legally important and politically responsible appeals, stretching from the time of the early church to the present that are considered here. These include actions without overt political intent such as that, for example, of the early Christian martyr Polycarp. Having rejected a Roman offer to spare his life if he would obey the law of Caesar, the old man's response was intensely spiritual. 'Eighty and six years have I served Him, and He never did me any injury: how then can I blaspheme my King and Saviour?'[8]

The model also includes the theo-political response of John Calvin. As able a lawyer as a Christian theologian, Calvin taught that obedience to superiors is restricted by the prior obligation of obedience to God, and insisted that should a law contradict the will of God it simply be allowed to go unesteemed. Calvin's perception of civil authority was, however, far more complex than this para-phrase of one section of the *Institutes* allows.[9] Michael Walzer has shown, for example, that the discontented of successive ages have seized on this and related comments in the closing part of the *Institutes* to generate a revolutionary political ethic which Calvin would probably have been reluctant to own.[10] Like other magisterial reformers, he held civil authority in high esteem: 'All those', he said, 'who have the right of the sword and public power are slaves of God even if they exercise tyranny and are brigands,' and he insisted that even an unjust ruler is sometimes raised up by God 'for the chastisement of the sinfulness of the people.'[11]

What distinguished Calvin from other magisterial reformers was his uncompromising affirmation of the theological principle (which at times contradicted his less systematic formulations on state obedience) of the direct and absolute sovereignty of God in Jesus Christ over all areas of life. Before this the claims of state, notions of the 'orders of creation', purity of race, ethnic identity or any other rival authority were rendered insignificant. By relating this understanding of divine sovereignty to a doctrine of covenant which incorporated the people of God into the redemptive work of God, Calvin imparted to the church, as an agent of God, responsi-bility to engage in transforming the social, political and economic structures of life.

Driven by this vision of a new social order, Calvin developed a more positive understanding of civil law than most other reformers, whose social pessimism caused them to regard law essentially as a means of punishing the wicked. For Calvin, law was an instrument of social justice and, it has been argued by some, his emphasis on the participation of all God's people in the formation of God's emerging new order constitutes a first cautious step towards a participatory democracy. As such Calvin anticipates the notion of law as an historical construction rather than a once-given divine reality.

Details aside, in Calvin's writings history probably acquired a more positive dimension than in any other major theologian in the tradition of the Christian church. For him nothing was left to chance. The sovereign God, in covenant with the people of God, was seen to shape, structure and determine the legal, political and indeed the entire social fabric of existence. And when this sovereign God is celebrated as a God who is, to quote Karl Barth, 'against the lofty and on behalf of the lowly; against those who already enjoy right and privilege and on behalf of those who are denied it and deprived of it', the revolutionary potential of the Calvinist model of law and politics is obvious. To continue with Barth, this is an ethic which requires the church to be against the reactionary, 'despite the wrongness of the revolutionary'.[12] It is an ethic not merely of abstract choice but rather an ethic of command experienced in the midst of one's own historical struggle, grounded in the concrete reality of the sovereign God having become the poor man of Nazareth.

When this ethic is appropriated within a particular context and by a particular people it constitutes a dynamic force in the process of law-making and political struggle. This is nowhere more clearly seen in the South African context than in the writing and ministry of Allan Boesak. The title of a collection of his essays places this in focus: *Black and Reformed*. 'Black' refers to the historical context of oppression in South Africa as seen from the perspective of op-pressed black people. 'Reformed' is an affirmation of the absolute sovereignty of God and the covenantal relationship between God and the people of God.[13] Facing a situation of oppression, Boesak employs those aspects of Calvin often neglected by institutional Reformed orthodoxy, reclaiming the traditional symbols of the Calvinist tradition in order to forge a theology that can withstand the tyranny of the South African regime. The consequence is a struggle for human dignity and political liberation in South Africa understood to be in continuity with that tradition of divine obedi-ence which has fuelled historically necessary political revolutions. Differently stated, the struggle for a liberated South Africa is seen, in the Calvinist model of law and politics, as a revolution within which God, in covenant with humankind, participates to bring about the redemption of the oppressed.

It is a tradition which has charged social reformers and sustained the oppressed throughout history. Barth employed it in rejecting Hitler's absolutist claims: 'No sentence', he said, 'is more dangerous than that God is One and there are no other like him... It was on the truth of the sentence that God is One that the "Third Reich" of Adolf Hitler made shipwreck'.[14] Dietrich Bonhoeffer, despite his high (classical Lutheran) regard for the state which convinced him as late as 1933 that the church could not 'exert direct political action', nevertheless conceded that in an extreme situation (when the state perverted its God-given authority) it was necessary for the church 'not just to bandage the victims under the wheel, but to put a spoke in the wheel itself....'[15]

Desmond Tutu affirms this tradition of divine obedience when he informs the South African government that, notwithstanding their power, they will end up as the 'flotsam and jetsam of history because the liberation God of the Exodus is always on the side of the underdog'. 'Mr Minister,' he told the Minister of Law and Order, 'we must remind you that you are not God. You are just a man. One day your name will merely be a faint scribble on the pages of history while the name of Jesus Christ, the Lord of the Church, shall live forever.'[16]

And more recently, when the Minister of Police warned clergy 'to toe the line', 'keep out of politics' and 'stick to the Christian message', Allan Boesak, in a sermon preached in St. George's Cathedral, told the Minister that Christians had only one 'line' to follow, that of obedience to God alone. 'You are not taking on individual Christians or ministers of the gospel,' he said, 'you are taking on God and any government which tries to do that cannot and will not survive.' 'To say that a government which knows no justice and denies human rights and dignity is illegitimate, *is* the Christian message,' he continued. 'In your denial of the Word of God and in your insistence on oppression ... you have ceased to be the servant of God. You have become the beast of destruction. To remind you of this, Mr Minister, *is* the Christian message.' Boesak's classical Calvinist revolutionary emphasis is most clear in the closing litany of his sermon:

Do what you like, Mr Minister, there is one thing the church knows: Jesus Christ is lord.

Threaten us and imprison us: Jesus Christ is lord.

Let your security police terrorise our children and threaten our lives: Jesus Christ is lord.

You may even choose to kill us, but the truth remains: Jesus Christ is lord.

Of course this tradition can be abused. Theologised Afrikaner nationalism is but one example of this. It is also an example of a nationalist option which has quite overtly turned away from a broad-based participatory democracy, which must always be given scope as a corrective to narrow or sectarian understandings of the divine will. This kind of abuse has persuaded some that Calvinism has worked better as a theology of politics outside of power than as an instrument of power. As 'an instrument that is a mighty weapon in warfare it may be an inconvenient tool for use in the building trade,' warned Paul Tillich.[17] The problem with successful revolutions is that those who tear down the structures of the old society are also required to share in the often ambiguous task of building the new. It is here that some forms of the model of law as divine obedience are most vulnerable, although Calvin's programme of social humanism in Geneva addressed the very issues faced in any contemporary phase of social reconstruction. Correctly understood, an ethic of divine obedience can also function as an instrument of continuing renewal or 'ongoing revolution', which is important for any state, however egalitarian or democratic.

Civil disobedience is an obvious and central tenet within this model of law. Laws which are seen to contradict the sovereign will of God are simply to be disobeyed. 'A just law is a man-made code that squares with the moral law or the law of God,' said Martin Luther King, while ' an unjust law is a code that is out of harmony with the moral law'.[18] Desmond Tutu has similarly argued: '... to fail to distinguish between morality and legality is immoral. To obey an immoral law is an immoral act.'[19]

A secular and milder equivalent of law as divine obedience is found in the liberal understanding of law as the articulation of natural or universal rights. More reflective of the contextual demands of each successive age, it is in some circles regarded as more appropriately equipped than a theory of divine obedience to serve the particular needs of societies at different periods of history. It is, however, precisely this reflection which allows it to be shaped and manipulated by the dominant forces of each successive age.

Law as social contract

The liberal contractual tradition of law which during the period of Enlightenment replaced the tradition of natural law is usually traced back to John Locke. It is a tradition of law developed in relation to a vision of rights regarded as anterior to and independent of any particular social order, although adopted in each successive age through the corporate will of the people. John Rawls, a modern proponent of the liberal tradition, argues that these rights are 'lexically prior' to the historical process, despite the appropriation of these rights by a particular people at a particular time.[20]

Within the context of this theory, civil disobedience finds its place where a given law is seen to be in violation of these rights. The contribution of individuals and communities within this tradition to the struggle for justice is well known. More inclusive and with wider appeal than liberal notions of human rights is, of course, traditional Catholic teaching on natural law as a means of human participation in *God's* eternal law for the world. There is an appealing constancy in the affirmation of such basic principles as human equality, dignity, justice, and truth. Such universal norms have, however, resulted in a plurality of interpretations. Moreover, in actuality the most hideous of social practices have been legitimated by an appeal to natural or divine law – although this particular model of law is by no means the only model within which such claims are made. 'God' has been used in various traditions to sanction numerous crimes against humanity!

The quest for an ideal that transcends social reality has not withstood the advent of the sociology of knowledge, which has shown that all ideas, however dialectically conceived, are linked to their social base. And when we consider Western liberal notions of rights, it is quite clear that these are defined in relation to specific historic bourgeois notions of human rights, including individual freedom and ownership of property, as proclaimed by Locke in England and Jefferson in America. Whatever one may think of these ideals in themselves one is hard pressed to show how the promotion of individual capitalist values is 'eternal' and 'natural' while support for communal and socialist ideals is not.

Liberal notions of human rights at times are also the source of social conservatism, lending support to a reactionary political stance. Robert Bellah has said that we live in a description of a place and not the place itself.[21] Persuaded that its perception of human rights is 'natural' and 'eternal', liberalism can provide a form of stubborn resistance to change. To the extent that it refuses to acknowledge that specific political influences shape these ideals, it can also be moralistic and authoritarian.

As a tradition, liberalism has nevertheless given rise to what Michael Walzer calls 'the heroic encounter between the sovereign individual and the sovereign state'.[22] Locke understood this well and regarded it as the right of a people to reclaim in revolution what they are deprived of by a tyrannous state.[23] Jefferson claimed that right on behalf of the American colonists stating that 'it is their right, it is their duty, to throw off [despotism]'.[24] The limitation of Lockean revolutionary theory, however, is that if only by default, it favours the established order. Locke realistically thought that 'the right to rebel will not easily engage them [the violated people] in a contest, wherein they are sure to perish', and warned that a revolution is only likely to succeed when it engages 'the whole body'.[25] Locke saw revolution to be a spontaneous popular combustion rather than a purposeful individual or group initiative for wider participation or rebellion against the political tyrant. He was infatuated with the possibilities of newly emerging liberal democratic action which became for him the major vehicle of political change. He played down the significance of civil disobedience but in theory allowed for its place within politics. Today liberals continue to allow for civil disobedience, but cling to the democratic process and the possibilities of the ballot box as the more likely vehicles of change in even the most oppressive situations.

This trust in the established political process is not, of course, limited to liberal societies. It is heralded as the motor of social transformation by the dominant classes of all societies. When the Christian church was elevated to a position of prominence with the Edict of Milan in 313 C.E., it too lost its earlier revolutionary zeal and opted for political compromise, as can be seen in the model of law to which we now turn.

Law as social realism

Augustine taught that a political order without justice was little more than a band of robbers, and projected a vision of 'the most glorious City of God' against which he measured the earthly city as it sighed and groaned while awaiting transformation. But ultimately he taught that earthly peace could be only partial and limited. It could be only the 'peace of Babylon' – something to be tolerated and endured until 'this mortal life shall give place to one that is eternal'. He separated the spiritual and political spheres of existence, and in so doing reduced history to a passing significance, exempted the state from the radical demands of the gospel and opened the door for the political compromise that has shaped the dominant tradition of the Christian church ever since.[26] Thomas Aquinas took the compromise further. He argued that 'an unjust law ... has the nature, not of law, but of violence', but ultimately allowed that it could well be in the interests of the common good that such a law be obeyed.[27] Like Augustine he argued that political realism required compromise.

Martin Luther thought that 'a wise prince is a mighty rare bird', and he warned the princes that the people would not endure their tyranny forever. If the rulers were to be obeyed in all things, he said, there would be no point in the scriptural injunction requiring that we obey God rather than human authority.[28] But ultimately Luther's two-kingdom doctrine anticipated an age of secular law-making, necessarily characterised by compromise and moderation. It is this which locates Luther within the tradition of 'Christian realism' as articulated by Augustine and Aquinas, rather than with the more militant model of radical divine obedience detected in parts of Calvin's writings.

A variety of circumstances and events shaped and nuanced Luther's teaching on law and civil disobedience. 'They are trying to make me a fixed star,' he said. 'I am an irregular planet!'[29] At times he was polemical and reactionary, as seen in his writings on the Peasants' Revolt of 1525, in his anti-Semitism and in his attitudes towards women. Few today would legitimate or defend his views on these matters.

Not uncritical of the princes, he nevertheless showed an understanding of the moral compromises, political deals and social necessities of political rule; and his theological legitimation of these acts contributed towards making him a trusted counsellor to three successive princes in Saxony. He believed in a natural hierarchical order and assumed that the German princes were the legitimate rulers of the day, well equipped 'to patch and darn as best we can while we live, punish abuses and lay bandages and poultices over the sores', within a temporal realm which, he believed, 'God does not think as much of as he does of the spiritual realm'.[30] This negative perception of the possibilities of significant social change is perhaps what distinguished Luther most clearly from Calvin. Those positive and optimistic views of government which are to be found at times in Luther's writings are left essentially undeveloped.[31]

For a variety of reasons (not least his location in society), Luther believed that the existing social order, despite its shortcomings, needed to be preserved. The only alternative to this order which he could imagine was chaos. In contrast, today many Christians in oppressive situations are persuaded that the existing order needs to be scrapped and that the prevailing rulers are themselves the source and cause of chaos. The militant Anabaptists of the sixteenth century thought more or less the same. These differences aside, Luther's perception of the political order as God's 'left hand' way of governance has given rise to a notion of law as the product of political negotiation and social realism, which makes sense to twentieth-century secular society. It is a theory of law which reminds us that politics is the art of the possible, and that the laws of the land *can* only be the product of political compromise. Indeed it is a theory of law which dismisses the imposition of moral absolutes in the political market-place as the tyranny of an idealism which society can scarcely afford. It makes an important contribution to Tillich's quest for a nation-building political ethic.

Law-making within this context insists that authentic Christian social ethics must be forged in and through the church's vigorous and continuous engagement with policy debates within the political community, but that the possibility of direct political engagement in the affairs of state should be excluded. The broad parameters of the political wisdom and theological necessity of this ethic are obvious. Two qualifications need, however, to be introduced:

1. For Luther the sphere of politics was essentially a secular one, while the ministry of the church was essentially spiritual. The importance of the two-kingdom doctrine in this regard lies in its insistence that politics must not be deified. It also teaches that even the most successful political orders need to be deabsolutised, judged and renewed in relation to God's kingdom, which is radically other than any kingdom humankind might build. The failure of the church in Nazi Germany to heed this lesson cost the Jewish people and the world more than humankind can ever again afford to pay. Moltmann's affirmation of Luther's two-kingdom doctrine as a 'critical-polemical separation between God and Caesar' is important in this regard.[32] Equally important, however, is the need to realise that the spiritual ministry of the church must be jealously defended against both those who seek to prescribe what may be preached within its limits and those who seek to prescribe its limits. Christian ministers are often obliged to transgress the stated limits of the Augsburg Confession, which is to 'preach the gospel and administer the sacraments'. In South Africa, for example, such limits are precisely those which the state is seeking to impose on the churches.[33]

2. Notions of realism beg the question concerning the nature of realism: Realism according to whom? The *Twelve Articles* containing the agrarian demands which culminated in the Peasants' Revolt of 1525 were realistic from the point of view of the peasants, but quite unrealistic for the princes, and when compelled to choose between peasants and princes Luther chose to side with the latter. A reviewer of Fox's biography of Reinhold Niebuhr, in commenting on Nie-

buhrian Christian realism, wisely noted, 'out of touch with reality, "realism" can go wrong'.[34] Such wisdom penetrates to the crux of too many manifestations of Christian realism. It is too frequently realism from the perspective of the dominant classes, articulated by those who befriend princes and presidents, rather than the realism of the poor. People intoxicated with the existing order do not need to see visions of a new order or dream dreams of a radically new age. They are content with the present. Vision, suggests Rubem Alves, is born of suffering and pain.[35]

To allow the laws of any nation to be little more than the crystallisation of bourgeois notions of what is possible is to deny the biblical vision of what God intends for creation. For Christians to allow their vision of social reality to be reduced to no more than this is to serve Caesar and not God. Laws which constrain us in this manner cause us to sin, and the consensus among Christians is that such laws must be disobeyed. The limitation of Niebuhr's Christian realism is that it tends to favour the rich and the powerful. Such notions are out of touch with the reality of the poor and oppressed and devoid of eschatological vision.

Law as political possibility

Political realism in its secular form is nowhere more clearly seen than in what is usually referred to as the conservative model of law. Sometimes referred to as the Whig model, it stands in the tradition of Edmund Burke, the conservative eighteenth-century English political philosopher.[36] It rejects all ideas of ideal or theoretical rights which claim to be independent of a particular society or 'lexically prior' to the historical process. Law is seen to be a human artifact. It is the slow sum of political bartering and compromise.

Law within this model is a symbol of the most fundamental historic values of a particular society – what Lord Devlin called a 'shared morality', which emerges over an extended period of time.[37] This conserving dimension of law consists of a political bias seen in the entrenched clauses of many Western constitutions. It is most vividly illustrated in the separation of powers in the United States constitution, by which the president, endowed with a power of veto, is required to safeguard certain historic values and ideals against the changing impulses of public opinion.

Law as political possibility is best understood by distinguishing between two usages of morality: *descriptive morality*, giving expression to the mores, customs and values of a particular society, and *normative morality*, referring to an ideal standard or norm against which to judge the particular behaviour of a society. 'Law as political realism' is an articulation of the mores (the descriptive morality) of the society of which it is a part.

As the dominant notion of law in the West, this kind of legal positivism is a tradition developed by the English Utilitarians, Jeremy Bentham and John Austin, and most clearly described in the writings of Hans Kelsen and H. L. A. Hart (whose theory of law is more extensively discussed in Chapter 5).[38] Within this tradition law does not cease to be a law simply because it violates some ideal or normative standard of morality. Austin wrote, 'the existence of law is one thing; its merits or demerits are another….'[39] Hans Kelsen argued that 'the validity of a legal norm cannot be questioned on the ground that its contents are incompatible with some [ideal] moral or [passing] political value'.[40]

Normative moral idealism is removed from this model of law, and biblical eschatological imperatives, however 'realistically' or 'moderately' interpreted, are rejected. Legal positivism is not, however, 'a command theory of law'. It is not, to quote Hart, 'the gunman situation writ large'.[41] Where there are bad laws these obviously need, according to legal positivists, to be changed – through political struggle and, according to Hart, 'if laws [have] reached a certain degree of *iniquity* then there would be a plain moral obligation to resist them and to withhold obedience'.[42] Edmund Burke could have written that sentence himself. Despite his high regard for law, he allowed for civil disobedience, as a legitimate and necessary means of opposing government.[43]

The pertinent question is by what criteria this moral judgment is to be made concerning the iniquity of any given law. The conservative political theory of law suggests that ultimately the criteria would be discerned within what we have already referred to as the alleged historic 'shared morality' of a given nation. Civil disobedience is justified, in other words, by the moral values which a particular law is supposed to promote.

Differently stated, the conservative model of law insists that the criteria against which the behaviour of individuals and groups within that nation be judged are to be found within the dominant morality of that nation. To link moral appeal to the dominant morality of an age or people is, however, to place the dissident at an unfair disadvantage in any attempt to vindicate herself or himself before a court of law. As such, civil disobedience is located at the edge rather than the centre of the political process. For this reason the alternative model of law defended especially by Lon Fuller is useful.

Law as moral incentive

This model of law, as a modern theory of natural law, affirms the presence of a normative moral foundation in law. It is most clearly illustrated in Lon Fuller's consideration of a society within which all traditional values, customs, moral imperatives and law-enforcement mechanisms have collapsed – a theory of law also discussed in Chapter 5.[44] He attempts hypothetically to reconstruct the primary state where, he suggests, the law-making function of a people is determined solely by certain 'innate' and 'natural' rights and values.[45]

It can, of course, be argued that these rights and values are a product of the struggle and conflict which brought a people to the point of law-making, and that they are not of a pre- or supra-historical kind. Be this as it may, Fuller's point ought not to be missed. He is *endeavouring* to overcome the trap into which conservative and traditional liberal political theories of law fall, which is to allow dominant forms of existing morality to be the judge of what is right and just. In reality it may not be possible to attain such normative purity. As a moral imperative it nevertheless constitutes an important incentive to transcend the demands of the dominant group within any society. Suffice it to say, Fuller relocates the option of civil disobedience at the centre of the legal system.

In summation, consideration has been given to five models of law:

1. Law as divine obedience.
2. Law as social contract.
3. Law as social realism.
4. Law as political possibility.
5. Law as moral incentive.

The attractiveness of models one and five – the latter at least as interpreted by Fuller – concerns the projection of an absolute God (in the case of model one) or norm (in the case of model two) as the final appeal against which to measure all law. The liberal tradition, as expressed in model two, is located in the same broad moral tradition although (as it has been argued above) in a more vulnerable way. The difficulty associated with these models concerns the understanding of the moral absolute in particular complex political situations. The sociological approach to morality and law poses an important challenge in this regard. It insists that ideas do not fall from the skies. They are dialectically shaped and structured by the social conflict and struggle from within which they emerge.

However, in a society where Machiavellian power politics is given precedence over moral concern, the quest for an absolute moral norm beyond the vicissitudes of social conflict is a powerful and heroic one which jurisprudence can scarcely afford to ignore.[46] The problem is that these models do not provide an immediately recognisable theoretical framework in terms of which to translate absolute ideals or principles into specific laws or political programmes. The historical character of law makes participatory democracy the only realistic hope for enduring justice and social renewal.

Model four addresses this need directly, but ultimately falters in allowing the parameters of morality to be limited and determined by those who win the political struggle for hegemony. Marx's axiom which suggests that the ruling ideas of any society (including ruling ideas about morality) are the ideas of the ruling class, is a sobering one – and all too often a fair description of the notions of morality which prevail in most legal systems.[47]

Model three allows, at the level of theory if not always of practice, for the interpretation and application of normative principles in relation to a specific political situation. Integral to this model is, however, the danger that the dominant social influences of the prevailing sectors of society will ultimately shape and give content to these principles. This stresses the importance of ideals beyond the dominant order of society, as articulated essentially in a theology of divine obedience and in the legal theory of Fuller. These are ideals which locate protest high on the political agenda of society, something that society can only afford to suppress only at its own peril.

The discussion on the 'ethics of last resort' in the Introduction is pertinent to the above discussion. Classical theological and philosophical notions of divine or natural laws have been questioned in the light of a sociological approach to morality which suggests that law is the product of social conflict and struggle. In what follows this insight is affirmed as axiomatic, but also affirmed are the interests of those often ignored in the resolution of conflict struggle – the 'nobodies' of society, the poor, oppressed and defeated. Civil disobedience and rebellion are often the only means by which such people can participate in the political process. To the extent that the church has an obligation to promote the interests of the oppressed it also has an obligation to legitimate theologically the location of such options at the centre of the political process, rather than at its extremities – and the demands of the oppressed are often articulated by way of civil disobedience. Civil disobedience is not necessary where alternative means of social transformation are possible. It is, however, a theologically legitimate form of activity where such alternatives do not exist. And in South Africa the poor and oppressed are denied democratic alternatives.

Civil disobedience as democratic action

Following the above, the need is for a model of law-making which takes secular politics seriously, while ensuring the right to dissent and resist as an important ingredient in the struggle against oppressive political hegemony. From the perspective of jurisprudence, Fuller's 'modern' natural law theory allows for dissent and resistance in a more viable manner than either the liberal model of law as social contract or the positivistic theory of law. From a theological perspective the quest is, in turn, for an option which combines political realism, as anticipated in Luther's theory of law, with a sense of revolutionary dissent and demand, as seen in Calvin's theory of law. Ignoring nuances and important qualifications, one could say that for Luther politics had to do with the *affairs of people*, whereas for Calvin politics concerned the *affairs of God.* The danger of Lutheran politics is that (despite Luther's safeguards) the separation of the two realms can turn religion into an other-worldly form of piety and politics into unbridled power-games. The danger of Calvinism (despite Calvin's awareness of such dangers) is the assimilation of religion and politics into a form of political messianism.

In nuanced form there is, on the other hand, a great deal of agreement between many of the formulations concerning the encounter between church and state in the writings of Luther and Calvin. Context does, however, influence one's way of doing theology. Luther, despite his many conflicts with the princes, was writing from the perspective of the rulers of the German elite, while Calvin was influenced by his location within a city of refugees.

The secular political process is today well established in most countries around the world. The right to dissent and resist is not. It is this, perhaps, which makes Calvin's teaching rather than Luther's more immediately and obviously applicable to the contemporary quest for social justice in situations of oppression – provided that the importance of his deabsolutising of the political process be kept in mind. Calvin's theology is primarily a theology of protest. It binds people in a covenant with God as a basis for transforming and renewing society, and this instinctively appeals where the oppressed are locked in conflict with the oppressor. It is an appeal which affirms conscientious objection as an important instrument of the oppressed in the struggle for justice and peace.

Closely related to the potential dangers perceived in the Calvinist and Lutheran models of law are the Burkean categories of 'intolerance and indifference' – which, Burke argued, are the twin evils of law and politics. The one concerns the tyrannical imposition of ruling ideas on those who dissent, and the other that brand of *laissez-faire* free market politics which 'indifferently' allows the strong to devour the weak.[48] It is the characteristic of the state, says Lord Devlin, to protect itself by law and to protect this law by force if necessary. If government is, however, to be more than tyranny, tolerance of dissent is a necessary ingredient of good government. There are for Devlin, however, limits beyond which dissent cannot go. 'A rebel', he argues, 'may be rational in thinking that he is right but he is irrational if he thinks that society can leave him free to rebel.'[49] As already indicated, Martin Luther King understood and accepted this injunction, while Edmund Burke insisted that civil disobedience, in the absence of viable alternative political options, is a regrettable but legitimate form of politics and law-making. Against sustained acts of civil disobedience and rebellion, he said, no ruler can govern except by suppression. And this, he insisted, is not government at all! A nation, he argued, 'is not governed, which is perpetually to be conquered'.[50]

The nature of politics is such that the strong dominate and the weak are dominated. Those who win ultimately write the rules about what constitutes fair play and morality. They even presume to interpret divine principles to favour their own cause.

In this situation principled and organised civil disobedience is very often the *only* channel through which the defeated and oppressed can share in the democratic process of political debate, consciousness-raising and law-formation. But such resistance requires moral legitimacy as a basis for countering the dominant morality of the oppressor. In a society where the victors have written the rules and within which God-talk is a dominant ingredient of culture and morality, a theology which favours the cause of the poor and oppressed is often not only the most potent, but at times the only, form of sanction available. It could well be said that, if an ethic of divine obedience providing a moral basis for resistance and civil disobedience did not exist, we would be obliged to create one. And, if it could not be argued from Scripture that God shows a preferential option for the poor (and the evidence for this is incontrovertible), it would be necessary to create such a God.

Civil disobedience in a country like South Africa, in the absence of free access to the ballot box, is among the few non-violent options available for direct participation in the democratic process. Its purpose is not to undermine true authority, nor to advocate anarchy. To quote from a statement of the Convocation of Churches which met in Johannesburg in May 1988 to devise ways of engaging in acts of non-violent resistance against the state: 'Rather, it is to distinguish between two different kinds of authority; legitimate authority which conforms to the truth of the gospel, and an illegitimate one which disregards the truth of the gospel.'[51]

If democracy is about participation, then, in the world of power-politics, civil disobedience is an inherent part of the democratic process. It invariably starts in a hesitant and cautious manner but, to the extent that it is suppressed by those who rule, to that extent does it intensify. The state, said Burke, is obliged to incorporate and conciliate those who rebel for conscience' sake. To fail to do so was, Burke thought, to invite others to join the protest, and 'I do not know a method', he said, 'of drawing up an indictment against a whole people'.[52] The failure by the state to deal creatively with civil disobedience is an invitation to revolution.

The failure of the South African state in this regard *explains the essence of* the revolutionary struggle in this country. The state's stubborn refusal to allow viable and realistic participation by blacks in the democratic process has provoked what has been called 'probably the largest grassroots eruption of diverse nonviolent strategies in a single struggle in human history'.[53] This eruption, which resulted in the banning of virtually all organisations that engage in viable forms of democratic protest and resistance, has been documented in Chapters 1 and 2.

Such acts of protest and civil disobedience are motivated and sustained by the innate conviction of a God-given right that the oppressed should be free. In secular parlance, protest is kept alive against the most sustained forms of repression by the belief in a tried and tested lesson of history which insists that some people can be oppressed for some of the time but not all people can be oppressed all of the time.

Where a regime refuses to allow itself to be changed by democratic means, it brings on itself that intolerable situation where (in the words of Burke) it seeks to impose an indictment on its own people. The message of history in this situation is unequivocal – the people respond in revolution.

Civil disobedience as revolutionary action

There is more at stake in the South African struggle for justice and peace than social reform. It is a struggle which involves not merely the scrapping of specific unjust laws. It involves the rejection of the total socio-economic and political structure – distinguishing the South African liberation struggle from the American civil rights campaign of the 1960s. This becomes clear in the *Theological Rationale* published by the SACC in 1985, calling the churches to pray for an end to unjust rule. The call is no longer for the reform of government but rather for qualitative change in the structures of government:

We have continually prayed for the authorities, that they may govern wisely and justly. Now, in solidarity with those who suffer most, in this hour of crisis we pray that God in His grace remove from His people the tyrannical structures of oppression and the present rulers in our country who persistently refuse to heed the cry for justice, as reflected in the Word of God as proclaimed through His church in this land and beyond.[54]

Similar sentiment is found in the *Kairos Document*: '... once it is established beyond doubt that a particular regime is tyrannical, it forfeits the moral right to govern and the people acquire the right to resist....'[55]

Reference has already been made to the tradition of political realism established by Augustine, sustained by Aquinas and developed by Luther, as a movement towards preventing the political order from becoming an entity in its own right. Well-entrenched through church–state conflicts in the medieval period, the separation of the 'spiritual' and 'political' orders became part of 'Western Christian Civilisation', and part of the dominant theological tradition of the church. Even in the Calvinist tradition, which insisted on the universal lordship of Christ over all creation, the political order eventually came to acquire a theological legitimacy of its own.

The church has nevertheless never managed to suppress a residual revolutionary theology (traceable back to the early church) which requires that it continually weigh the existing order against the demands of God's impending kingdom. This is what Johann Baptist Metz calls the 'dangerous memory' which contradicts the church's social location in society. It is an *alternative* Christian tradition adjacent to the dominant tradition (Augustine would say the two traditions 'commingle' in history), seen in Augustine's rejection of unjust rulers as a band of robbers and in Aquinas's insistence on the obligation of Christians to resist tyranny. It is also present in Luther's insistence that there are limits beyond which civil authority cannot be permitted to go, and in Calvin's affirmation of the lordship of Christ over every sphere of human existence. This is a tradition which insists that when a regime has become *hostis boni communis*, the enemy of the common good, in an enduring and persistent manner, it is the obligation of the church to resist and oppose such a regime as being a tyrant and enemy of God.[56]

The *Concise Oxford Dictionary* defines tyranny as 'the despotic or cruel exercise of power', and the tyrant as 'an oppressive or cruel ruler; a person exercising power arbitrarily or cruelly'. It is the obligation of the church to oppose such rule as rebellion against God and a violation of God's people. 'South Africa is a textbook case of a tyrannical regime hostile to the interests of the majority of its people,' argues Albert Nolan.[57]

A tyrannical state has suppressed virtually all forms of democratic protest in South Africa. It has acted against the mildest forms of conscientious objection, outlawed all options for civil disobedience as a means of political action within the broader structure of the rule of law, and systematically violated the tenets of its own legal heritage. It is this that requires the church, obligated as it is to proclaim liberty to the captives and to set the oppressed people free (Luke 4: 18), to move beyond protest and to engage in the struggle of the people to remove the present regime from power.

Context has always shaped theology. State oppression and repression in South Africa have provided the social context for a revolutionary theology. It is a theology which, in subjecting all forms of human authority to the radical demands of God's kingdom, draws on the 'dangerous memory' of the gospel which requires Christians to resist all forms of evil and injustice. It is a theology encapsulated in the statement of the Convocation of Churches to which reference has already been made:

We dare not be overcome by impotence, nor is confession of sin sufficient. We are called to repentance, relocating ourselves on the side of those who suffer most – in resistance, action, intercession and compassionate solidarity.

Called to proclaim and witness to truth in living, and even by dying, we now commit ourselves with solemn resolve in prayer and action to end unjust rule in our country and to see the advent of a democratic society of justice and peace.[58]

On deabsolutising law

We conclude where this chapter began. 'Law' is a powerful symbol in the struggle for social justice. Grounded in a morality which transcends the interests of the dominant classes and protects the rights of the poor and oppressed, it can be a powerful instrument of justice and peace. It can also be a symbol of oppression used by the dominant classes to oppress the poor. As such it can be a misleading symbol of subterfuge.

Every society needs laws to protect its people. When laws are unjust and a violation of the common good, they must be opposed. When the state itself is unjust, it must be totally rejected. In the South African context, the focus has moved beyond opposition to specific laws not only to a removal of a specific government from power but to a rejection of the prevailing oppressive nature of the existing state itself. It is this that makes the distinction which academics identify between 'government' and 'state' of little importance in the present South African context. The very system of rule and all that constitutes an oppressive 'state' are upheld by the present government, and the rejection of the one cannot be separated from that of the other. 'Disturbing such a government', said the less than radical Aquinas, 'has not the nature of sedition... . Indeed it is the tyrant rather that is more guilty of sedition....'[59] An inevitable question in this regard is whether it is theologically legitimate for Christians to resort to violence in order to remove the tyrant. To this question we now turn.

4
War, tyranny and revolution

The choice in South Africa is no longer a simple choice between violence and non-violence or between war and peace. Violent confrontation between oppressor and oppressed is already a daily reality. In this chapter the question is asked whether it is theologically legitimate for the oppressed to resort to violence as a means to defend themselves against the violence of the state.

'Violence' is a word used selectively in South African state propaganda. News reports, for example, tell us: 'Police were compelled to use force to counter the violence of stone-throwing youths....' 'Police were forced to use teargas and birdshot to restrain student violence at the University of Cape Town.' 'The police used rubber bullets to prevent further outbreaks of township violence....'

For this reason the *Kairos Document*, written in response to the intensification of civil war in South Africa, rejects the 'blanket condemnation of all that is called violence'.

The problem ... is the way the word violence is being used in the propaganda of the State. The State and the media have chosen to call violence what some people do in the townships as they struggle for their liberation, that is, throwing stones, burning cars and buildings and sometimes killing collaborators. But this excludes the structural, institutional and unrepentant violence of the State and especially the oppressive and naked violence of the police and army. These things are not counted as violence. And even when they are acknowledged to be 'excessive', they are called 'misconduct' or even 'atrocities' but never violence. Thus the phrase 'violence in the townships' comes to mean what the young people are doing and not what the police are doing or what apartheid is doing to people.[1]

In state propaganda, but sometimes also in theological debate, revolutionary violence is blamed for repressive violence. Ironically the oppressed are held responsible for the brutality they suffer at the hands of the police and army. Of course not all violence by oppressed people is revolutionary violence. Violence of different

kinds is just below the surface in most societies and perhaps especially among the oppressed, but as discussed in the Introduction it
is not easy to distinguish between 'revolutionary' and 'indiscriminate' violence. *Revolutionary* violence is, nevertheless, invariably a
response to the violence of state and institutional oppression.

Edmund Burke's recognition that any regime must come to
terms with democratic protest and civil disobedience, has been
noted in the last chapter. It is in the regime's self-interest to do so.[2]
The tragedy is that the South African regime has deliberately and
brutally repressed acts of protest and civil disobedience. It has
criminalised a variety of expressions of political protest, and persuaded large sections of the oppressed community seriously to
consider revolutionary violence as the only option available for
effective political transformation.

The criminalisation of political protest

The politics of resistance and revolutionary struggle in South Africa
cannot be understood apart from the criminalisation of meaningful
democratic political protest by parliament and the courts. This
process has been outlined in Chapter 2.

One consequence (and there are many others) of this process is
the extraordinarily high number of 'criminal' and 'political' prisoners or detainees in South Africa. At times it is difficult to distinguish
between what is a criminal offence and a political act, with children
of twelve years and under having been convicted of 'public violence'
and 'malicious damage to property' for throwing stones at armed
vehicles or painting slogans on buildings. The now restricted Detainees' Parents Support Committee (DPSC) estimated that between the declaration of the present state of emergency and
September 1987 over 30 000 political detainees had seen the inside
of South African prisons, with between 30 per cent and 40 per cent
of these being between the ages of 10 and 18 years. Some time after
these figures were released, the Minister of Justice confirmed that,
on 31 December 1987, 210 children of 15 years, 995 youths of 16
and 17 years of age and 6 277 youths of 18 and 19 years were in
prison awaiting trial or sentence for a variety of criminal and
political offences.

A series of hunger strikes by detainees and other forms of
political action have resulted in the release of significant numbers
of detainees and prisoners but many still remain in jail or are
restricted. The historic repression of protest has also created a

culture of alternative forms of resistance which is not likely to change radically prior to the institution of the process of democratic rule.

Revolution as a response to state tyranny

History would seem to suggest that the will to political liberation is almost as inherent in what it means to be human as the will to life itself. Sustained oppression and imposed servitude have inevitably given rise to protest, resistance and revolution. The history of South Africa is no exception.[3]

When normal democratic channels are denied to people in quest of freedom, and non-violent forms of conscientious objection are repressed, armed struggle tends to become the next costly but (from the perspective of the oppressed) logical, necessary and justified step. This is a position which can be questioned by only the most dedicated of pacifists, and history is cluttered with examples of those who have resorted to arms for less noble causes.

This much is confirmed in the story of Afrikaner history as portrayed in the Voortrekker Monument in Pretoria. Here the Boer soldiers with rifle, horse and Bible are revered symbols of white determination to dominate a black majority. There is also the idealised memory of the two Anglo–Boer wars fought in the name of justice and liberation despite the oppression and exploitation of the indigenous population within both the Boer republics and the British colonies. But this celebration of violence is not the unique possession of the Afrikaner. The British have their own memorials in the form of blood-stained battle colours, the Union Jack and the cross in 'English' churches throughout the Eastern Cape. Here the British soldier who fought and died for God, Queen and country in imperial endeavour is held up as an example for all to follow.

Black tribes obviously resisted the occupation of their land by Boer and Brit alike and were ultimately defeated by superior gun power. Black resort to revolutionary violence in the present century has, however, been slow and reluctant. This much is established in the early historical chapters of this study. It is a history well summarised in the speech of Nelson Mandela at his trial in 1962.

They [the white government] set the scene for violence by relying exclusively on violence to meet our people and their demands.... We have warned repeatedly that the government by resorting continuously to violence, will breed, in this country, counter-violence amongst the people, till ultimately, the dispute between the government and my people will finish up being settled in violence and by force.[4]

The state had created the conditions of revolution. The oppressed people responded. This is how oppressed people perceive the struggle, and it is important that this perception be emphasised in a situation where the dominant view of the present conflict is shaped by state propaganda.

Some theological aspects of the violence debate

In situations of sustained repression, revolution is historically inevitable, and debate on the morality of revolution is perhaps as pointless as a discussion on the morality of a natural disaster. The church nevertheless has grappled from its earliest days with questions of violence and insisted on ethical rules for war.

Each age has raised its own questions about violence in response to the different demands and crises of the time.[5] The early church, for example, expected God's kingdom to dawn imminently amidst the affairs of humankind, while it faced a hostile government determined to eradicate Christianity as a subversive influence in the Roman Empire. For early Christians the pertinent question was whether or not they were justified in taking up arms, either in self-defence or in the service of the state. In the post-Constantinian era, on the other hand, Christians readily fought for the Empire under the insignia of Christ. For the church within this period the most important theological question had changed. It was no longer a question of whether it was permissible to fight but a question of what constituted a just war. A theological imperative was the establishment of criteria in terms of which a distinction could be made between wars with a just (or, as some prefer to say, a 'justified') cause and end, and wars of material greed, national pride, vindictiveness, power and the like. And soon a related question emerged concerning the responsibility of Christians regarding tyrannical rule. To what extent were they permitted or obligated to resort to arms to remove the tyrant?

The church in South Africa today faces all of these issues anew. White conscripts to the army ask whether it is theologically legitimate for them to fight in the South African Defence Force. The military occupation of Namibia, cross-border raids and war in the townships have been weighed up in terms of traditional just war theory, and theology being rewritten from the perspective of the oppressed is rediscovering the significance of traditional theological teaching on tyrannical rulers. Concerns such as these are making the struggle in South Africa a theological as well as a political conflict, prompting a confrontation which could locate the present church–state conflict in South Africa as one of the most important of the present century. To a consideration of these issues we now turn.

Just war theory

The dominant teaching of the mainline churches concerning war and violence today continues to be traditional just war theory, which in its classical form is traced back to the Roman orator and statesman Cicero (d. 43 B.C.E.). Ambrose of Milan (c. 339–397 C.E.) introduced Cicero's ideas into Christian theology, subsequent church fathers such as Augustine and Thomas Aquinas entrenched them as a part of the Christian ethos, and Luther and Calvin carried them into the Protestant Reformation.

Each of these writers gave the doctrine of just war different emphases. These are important variations in the historical tradition of the church which has at times operated firmly in the service of the rulers and at other times struggled to distance itself from oppressive rulers by affirming an alternative liberative tradition. What follows offers no more than the essential emphases of just war theory.[6]

1. There must be a *just cause*.

Augustine thought that 'a just war is justified only by the injustice of an aggressor', suggesting that a just war is essentially a defensive war.[7] He went further, however, to allow that a just war could also be an aggressive war, arguing that a just cause for war could include the restoration of 'what was taken unjustly'.[8] Confronted with the plunder and carnage of his time, he was concerned to limit war, but he allowed that in a less than ideal situation war might need to be waged for a just cause and in pursuit of a just end.

Martin Luther similarly held that war is like a plague and that if aggressive wars are of the devil, defensive wars are human disasters. Most wars, he thought, were waged for the wrong reasons: selfishness, anger, lust for power and the desire for glory, but he allowed that as it was right for a ruler to punish a thief and a murderer, so it was right that war be declared on 'a whole crowd of evildoers' or an aggressive state. He said in such situations that the soldier's 'slaying and robbing' should be called 'works of love'! Such works, he said, are 'precious and godly'.⁹ Like Luther, Calvin thought war could be allowed only as a means to ensure peace and social stability – but he took the argument a cautious step further, allowing that if a ruler was responsible for chaos and injustice within a state, rebellion against such a ruler (provided it was led by a magistrate or secondary public figure) was permissible.¹⁰ To such matters we return. Childress has summarised the 'just cause' criterion well. It could be reasonably argued, he writes, that this involves the protection of the innocent from unjust attack, the restoration of rights wrongly denied a people and the re-establishment of a just order.¹¹ Briefly stated, a 'just cause' has come to be regarded as the redressing of an unjust situation.

2. There must be a *just end*.

Closely related to the concept of a 'just cause', the object of war should be the restoration of a just and lasting peace.

Some have interpreted this criterion to mean that where the cost of war in terms of human suffering is exorbitant, without some clear indication of likely victory and consequent peace, such a war perhaps ought not to be fought. For them it involves the question whether the likely outcome of the war warrants the kind of price it is likely to exact in terms of life and property. More broadly stated, the question concerns the likelihood of 'success.' Others, Karl Barth among them, while affirming the need to focus on justice and peace as the ultimate goal of war, argue that where a person or a community believes before God that a war needs to be fought, the cost cannot be regarded as a decisive factor.¹²

The assessment of the cost of war or an evaluation of possible future misery is, of course, always relative to a given situation. To state the obvious, blacks and whites in South Africa would 'read' cost and end differently. And the tragedy is that the suffering of the oppressed is sometimes such that they cannot imagine a future suffering worse than their present ordeal. Indeed history suggests that some prefer anarchy to continued oppression and it may be that oppression has to drive people to this kind of desperation before revolution is possible. The point of this particular criterion is, however, a rather simple one – namely, that a just end involves having peace and justice as a goal, rather than mere vengeance or the satisfaction of the lust for power.

3. *Just means* ought to be used.

This criterion implies some relationship between means and end. It requires restraint in the choice of weapons with a view to minimising suffering and death as well as the atrocities of war. The Geneva Convention (1949) and two subsequent 1977 Geneva Protocols are, for example, in accordance with this criterion in seeking to prohibit 'direct intentional attacks on non-combatants and non-military targets', arguing for the banning of nuclear arms, and seeking to prohibit the use of torture.[13] In guerilla warfare this criterion raises important questions concerning armed attacks on civilian and 'soft' targets.

In South Africa, despite the loss of civilian lives, guerilla attacks have been primarily state-aimed, at police and military institutions and installations. Recently however, there have been some attacks on shopping-centres and other public places, raising the question whether the African National Congress has changed its earlier commitment not to strike at non-combatants or non-military and non-strategic targets. A recent response by ANC President Oliver Tambo warned that the officials of apartheid were to be regarded as targets and that combat situations might arise in which civilians could be caught in the crossfire. Whatever one's assessment of this situation, the observation by Archbishop Desmond Tutu in March 1987 is revealing: '... Mr Tambo could quote broad statistics that the ANC had caused 80 deaths from 1976 to 1984, and the security forces had been responsible for 2 000 deaths since 1984.'[14]

Perhaps the criterion of just war theory requiring 'just means' is the most difficult of all the criteria to put into practice in the heat of battle. It is, however, an important appeal for restraint.

4. War must be a *last resort.*

All other means are to be tried and tested before the resort to force can be regarded as justifiable. For many it is this criterion which constitutes the most important emphasis of just war theory. It is a dominant criterion. If war be anything other than a last resort, even if all other criteria apply, it is generally regarded neither as justified nor as being just.

5. War must be declared by a *legitimate authority.*

The dominant tradition of the Christian church, at least since the time of Constantine, has shown a consistent bias in favour of the *de facto* rulers. Fearing the possibility of anarchy and chaos, the church has resisted armed revolution. It is also clear, however, that if all *de facto* governments are to be regarded as synonymous with legitimate authority, resistance to tyranny could never be accept-able. Yet Augustine and Thomas Aquinas, as major proponents of just war theory, and Luther and Calvin as their Protestant counterparts, agree that the time comes when the tyrant should no longer be obeyed. They further agree that in one way or another, if it be the will of God, the tyrant will be removed. Precisely who is responsible for this removal and by what means is a question to which we return.

Debate on the just war theory continues and clearly it can be used and abused (as it has been throughout history) to legitimate wars of both oppression and anarchy. When honestly employed, however, it can provide a useful framework for analysing situations of potential warfare. It is a theory of reluctant violence, but also one which allows that war is sometimes not only inevitable but perhaps necessary. More important for the South African situation is, however, the question of tyranny and whether theologically it is legitimate to resort to armed struggle in removing the tyrant.

Tyranny

The broad consensus within the church concerning the obligation of individuals and communities to resist tyranny has already been explained in the previous chapter. It is summarised in Luther's simple observation: '… if we are to do everything that temporary authority wanted there would have been no point to say, "We must obey God rather than men."'[15] In the words of Aquinas, 'A tyrannical government is unjust because it is not directed to the common good.' 'Disturbing such a government', he said, 'has not the nature of sedition.…'[16] Christian teaching concerning tyrants is ambivalent in places, but ultimately allows that, where a government acts in contradiction to the common good and in violation of the laws of God, it should be disobeyed. The question is whether it is legitimate for Christians to remove the tyrant by violence.

Augustine never doubted that a state devoid of justice and sustained by violence could not survive the exigencies of history. This, he argued in the *City of God*, was the reason for the fall of the Roman Empire. At the same time, however, he insisted that it was not the primary responsibility of Christians to concern themselves with such temporal matters. Aquinas rejected the possibility of ordinary citizens involving themselves in armed rebellion against the tyrant, while granting that in their obedience to God they may well find themselves martyred by the state. He also, however, allowed that God might see fit to remove the tyrant in some other manner. 'The government of tyrants … cannot last long,' he said. 'Those who are kept down by fear will rise against their rulers if the

opportunity ever occurs when they can hope to do it with impunity.'
Realistic enough to recognise that sooner or later an oppressed
people will rise up in rebellion against a tyrant, he also (as already
noted) refused to regard such action as seditious. Aquinas was
nevertheless reluctant to advocate or support such an initiative by
the oppressed.[17]

Luther's teaching showed a similar emphasis to that of Aquinas.
Should the tyrant command what is contrary to the will of God, he
should be disobeyed, with the sure expectation that such a ruler
would be dealt with according to the will of God.[18] The implication
is clear. The tyrant may well be overthrown or removed from office
in some other way, but Luther was not ready to permit his followers
to involve themselves in this activity. Calvin, as already indicated,
allowed that under a recognised leader in government (a magistrate) the common people could legitimately rise in rebellion. He
continued to insist, however, in the tradition of his predecessors,
that this was not an excuse for the common people to take this
initiative themselves.[19]

A rather strange situation had emerged within the dominant
tradition of the church. Christians were taught not to involve
themselves in violent revolution against a tyrannical government,
even while theologians accepted that other members of the community could be relied on to do so! Augustine, Aquinas and Luther
refused to provide theological legitimation for revolution, while
their political realism set the stage for later developments in this
regard. Calvin went a cautious step further in allowing for revolution under the leadership of a magistrate. The sluice-gate was
slowly being opened (in a way that Calvin probably never anticipated) making it justifiable for oppressed people to argue that a
different category of leadership might in different situations legitimately exercise this important responsibility assigned to the magistrates in Geneva. Calvin's point was that those entrusted with
protecting the rights of the populace, who in Geneva at the time
were the 'magistrates', had an obligation in extreme situations to
lead the people in opposition and possibly in revolution against the
ruler of the time.

'In South Africa,' said a black Christian standing within the
Calvinist tradition, 'it is our legitimate community leaders who are
required to protect our rights and lead us in such actions as may be
necessary to ensure that the present unjust rulers are removed from
power.' Theodore Beza, Calvin's successor in Geneva, went beyond

Calvin in legitimating revolution, and, in the turbulent history of religious wars and rebellion that followed, much of the caution of earlier ages was thrown to the wind.[20]

The *ancien regime*, within which the ruler found a location under God, was beginning to crumble, and as the long and slow shift towards the participation of the common people in government gained momentum, so these rights came to include the right to rebel against the tyrant. In brief, it was assumed that, where the means to remove a tyrannical government by peaceful means was denied a people, they had the right to do so by force. The theological contours of this debate were extensive and varied. They ranged from Zwinglian theological notions of legitimate war and the exploits of Thomas Münzer, Carlstadt and the Zwickau prophets to Oliver Cromwell, who believed that 'he who prays best fights best', and John Knox, who insisted that to remain silent in the face of tyranny was tantamount to complicity with the tyrant.[21]

There is but a short step from theologically allowing for rebellion to theologically instigating holy war. It is this which has obliged the church to integrate its teaching on tyrannical rule with its teaching on just war theory. It is this integration which stands central to theo-political debate in numerous Third World situations today.

The theology of just war was originally written from the perspective of the dominant classes of society. Rewritten from the perspective of the poor and oppressed, just war theory acquires the character of a theology of just revolution, becoming an important instrument in evaluating the legitimacy of revolution. Traditionally just war theory was intended to limit war between nations, and as a theory of just revolution it should legitimately be used in the same restraining manner. Traditionally it allowed that in certain extreme situations war might be justified even if never entirely 'just' or 'good'; as a theory of revolution it also allows that revolution, under certain circumstances, might be justified.

It is within this framework that Pope Paul VI in *Populorum Progressio* (1967) discouraged revolutionary uprisings, while allowing for an exception. 'Everyone knows', he said, 'that revolutionary uprisings – *except where there is manifest, longstanding tyranny which would do great damage to fundamental personal rights and dangerous harm to the common good of a country* – engender new injustices, introduce new inequities and bring new disasters.'[22] A year later, with the same reserve, Pope Paul VI told the Latin American bishops meeting in Medellin that, while a 'revolution is an unacceptable remedy for justice because it gives rise to worse evils', there might be exceptions to this general guideline. Reflecting the revolutionary milieu of the Latin American continent, the statement of the Medellin Conference drew on the pope's observation but ultimately revealed a different emphasis. The pope saw revolutionary violence as essentially unacceptable, while allowing that there might be certain rare exceptions to this rule. The Medellin Document, on the other hand, first stressed that revolutionary insurrection can sometimes be legitimate, while allowing that revolution can give rise to its own set of injustices.[23] The 1986 Vatican *Instruction*, in turn, warns against the 'mystique of violence' in condemning what it regards as the destructive illusion of 'systematic violence put forward as a necessary path to liberation'. It nevertheless allows that 'in the extreme case' armed struggle is allowed for by the church's magisterium as a means 'to put an end to an obvious and prolonged tyranny'.[24]

Speaking from within the just war tradition, President Kenneth Kaunda suggests in a poignant way the limits of revolutionary violence by arguing that violence is at best a *first step* in the process of building a just order. But as a *last resort* it may be an unavoidable step towards the pursuit of this order.[25]

In summation: the dominant tradition of the church allows the resort to violence by rulers under certain circumstances. And in more recent times, owing to the challenge presented by situations of oppression in different parts of the world, together with theological insights gained within these situations, the bias which allowed only the *de facto* rulers to take up arms legitimately has been broadened to allow for the common people to resort to arms against longstanding tyranny. The very concept of 'legitimate authority' is under new consideration at present and just war theory has come to provide a theoretical understanding of the concept of a just revolution.

As early as 1970 the World Council of Churches argued that the oppressed people of southern Africa had themselves concluded that the time for armed struggle had come, and that this meant that those not directly involved in that struggle were in no position to insist that the 'last resort' had not been reached or that the oppressed should continue to seek alternative ways to liberation.[26] More recently, some Christians went a step further to state in the *Lusaka Statement* of May 1987: 'While remaining committed to peaceful change we recognise that the nature of the South African regime which wages war against its own inhabitants and neighbours compels the movements to use force along with other means to end oppression.'[27]

Cautiously phrased, this statement is the closest Christians have come in a formal statement towards legitimating the armed revolutionary struggle in South Africa. It does not explicitly employ just war theory in support of the armed struggle; it does, however, come close to doing so.

In reopening the theological debate on violence, and in challenging the churches to move beyond the naïve rejection of all violence in a country already engulfed in violence, the theology of such documents as the *Lusaka Statement* and the *Kairos Document* is in continuity with a long theological tradition and in sympathy with a broad alliance of Christians around the world. It is a theology which challenges Christians to ask which form of violence is less evil: violence as a means of oppression or violence employed as a counter-strategy of liberation?

Is there an alternative to armed revolution in South Africa?
A statement made by Archbishop Desmond Tutu, expressed during a visit to Mozambique in 1987, is close to that of the *Lusaka Statement*.

We regard all violence as evil.... This does not mean, however, that the mainstream tradition of the church does not reluctantly allow that violence may in certain situations be necessary. The just war theory makes this point clearly.
... The Allies argued that it was justifiable, indeed obligatory to go to war to stop Hitler's madness, and the church concurred with that decision. Most people (apart from the purest pacifists) knew in their bones that it was right to fight against Nazism.
This is a situation which causes much puzzlement in the black community. Not only did the Allies go to war against Hitler with the approval of the church, but the church aided underground resistance movements which operated in Nazi-occupied countries.... More than this, most Western countries have their independence written in blood. The USA became independent after thirteen colonies had fought the American War of Independence. But when it comes to the matter of black liberation the West and most of its church suddenly begins to show pacifist tendencies.[28]

South Africa is not likely to escape the cycles of repressive and revolutionary violence before it learns to live in peace. Military and police spokespersons have repeatedly warned the oppressed people who resist apartheid that they have experienced only the beginning of what the South African police and military are capable. The truth of the matter is that armed revolutionaries have also been restrained. A former foreign correspondent of the *New York Times,* Joseph Lelyveld, suggests that the ANC must be numbered among the world's 'least effective' liberation movements.[29] If efficacy is measured in terms of violence (and one would hope not) this may well be true!

The consequences of escalating violence by either side are great in magnitude. John Vorster (a former South African prime minister) suggested that the very thought of total war is 'too ghastly to contemplate' – so ghastly that some who have never shown pacifist tendencies before are suddenly looking to this tradition as the only viable solution to an intensified spiral of violence.

Pacifism

As a doctrine which continues to disturb the conscience of the church, reminding it of that self-understanding which controlled its destiny during its earliest years, pacifism must continue to haunt the church.

Some find it difficult to affirm pacifism in principle, not wanting to rule out the possibility of resorting to arms in certain extreme circumstances while honouring non-violence as normative practice for the Christian. Others who are convinced pacifists know that the early church was also a church of the poor and oppressed, and that until such time as the present-day church is willing to share in the suffering of the poor, becoming a church of the poor, it is in no position to instruct oppressed people on how to respond to sustained violence and tyranny. Yet even those whose understanding of the political process leaves them unable to affirm pacifism in any way are obliged to take it seriously, because of the normative character for the Christian church of the New Testament witness to the non-violent life and ministry of Jesus. When, in turn, it is acknowledged that the resort to violence has often resulted in further misery rather than an improvement in the quality of life of those involved, war and revolution cannot be condoned as anything other than a desperate last resort – what Barth called a Grenzfall situation.[30]

The spiral of violence continues to escalate throughout the world, primarily in Third World countries forced to fight not only their own wars but also by proxy the wars of others. A realistic reading of history, however, tells us that the time comes for oppressed people when they would rather embrace such forms of violence than settle for further oppression. And it may be that Christians are ultimately required to judge violence less harshly than indifference, if only because the latter can never be an instance of love.

Can the spiral of violence be broken?

The elimination of violence is directly related to the elimination of state and institutional oppression. This is seen nowhere more clearly than in a rare exchange of views between P. W. Botha and Nelson Mandela in 1985. Botha offered Mandela his freedom on condition that he reject violence as a political instrument. 'I am surprised at the conditions that the government wants to impose on me,' Mandela replied. 'It was only when all other forms of resistance were no longer open to us that we turned to armed struggle. Let Botha show that he is different to Malan, Strijdom and Verwoerd. Let him say he will dismantle apartheid.... Let him guarantee free political activity so that the people may decide who will govern them.'[31]

General Coetzee, the former head of the South African Police, seemed to miss this point, when, in an affidavit to the Supreme Court designed to vilify alleged ANC supporters, he quoted Oliver Tambo's speech at the 75th anniversary celebrations of the African National Congress: 'The need to take up arms will never transform us into prisoners of the idea of violence, slaves of the goddess of war. And yet, if the opponents of democracy have their way, we will have to wade through rivers of blood to reach the goal of liberation, justice and peace.'[32]

There is an alternative to the armed struggle. It involves the democratic process, and it is essential that the South African rulers allow this to be the alternative to an armed struggle. The question is how democratic forces inside South Africa and in the international community can combine to ensure that the present regime is brought to an end. It is this situation which is addressed by Archbishop Tutu in the Mozambique speech to which reference has already been made:

International action and international pressure are among the few non-violent options left. And yet how strident is the opposition to economic sanctions. Blacks cannot vote. We are driven therefore to invoke a non-violent method which we believe is likely to produce the desired result. If this option is denied us, what then is left? If sanctions should fail there is no other way but to fight.[33]

What, then, is expected of the institutional church in the event of its deciding that the time to fight has come? Does the Archbishop become a General? Hopefully not! The question concerning the 'last resort' is important but, *in terms of practical institutional church options*, it does not address the responsibility of the church. The church's theological response to revolutionary violence is one thing, its practical response to a situation of oppression is another (a matter considered in Chapter 5).

The nervous energy expended by the institutional churches in debating the morality of revolutionary violence constitutes at best a serious waste of time (with few taking ecclesial verdicts on such matters too seriously!) and at worst an act of theological subterfuge, enabling them to escape their obligation to share in the struggle for the liberation of the oppressed. Given its calling to proclaim liberty to the captives and to set the oppressed free, the church can best contribute to the elimination of violence by engaging in whatever actions it may deem theologically acceptable to change the prevailing situation of oppression, but it must do something!

The church in South Africa has never seriously explored non-violent options, which do *not* offend its sensitivities regarding revolutionary violence. Frank Chikane has argued that the space which some have in which to talk about non-violence and even to engage in some forms of non-violent action is a space which has already been taken away from black township dwellers. For them there is 'time only for responding to the violence of the system'. Faced with this situation, they are obliged to 'either run for [their] lives or fight back in self-defence' – and an increasing number are refusing to run.[34] Theologically in no position to pass judgment on or to condemn such people, the church is obliged to use and seek to expand the space at its disposal to eliminate the violence of apartheid which obliges some people to become revolutionaries, thus preventing them from spending their energies in the more creative and pleasing activities for which God created humankind.

History is not likely to judge the churches for failing to provide theological legitimation for the armed struggle. Future generations might even condemn any such legitimation, if this were to be used as a basis for legitimating revolution in less extreme (*Grenzfall*) situations. These future generations will, however, be justified in asking what serious alternatives were engaged in by the church to bring the present regime to an end.

Beyond theology

Paul Lehmann has persuasively argued that, when a state persistently turns away from the options presented it for non-violent solutions, the patience of the people and the control of their leaders collapse – and apocalyptic violence explodes.[35] In the absence of imaginative compromises by the state, South Africa could find itself thrust into such a situation. It is this that obligates the church to discern alternative means to bring about the end to unjust rule.

The debate on violence, but also on non-violent strategies for qualitative political change, is ultimately a debate which takes place beyond theology and at the level of social analysis. The 1986 Vatican *Instruction* is clear: 'the concrete application of ... [the right to an armed struggle] cannot be contemplated until there has been a *very rigorous analysis of the situation*'.[36] The major division within the church occurs in relation to this analysis. Socio-economic and political divisions within the church render it incapable of a common diagnosis of the problem. Even more disconcerting is the fact that many of those who have condemned apartheid most strongly in verbal terms have good reason not to support the demise of the present order.

Simply put, not everyone in South Africa or beyond its borders agrees that its *kairos* has come. Some within the country and some within the Western capitals continue to look for partial and less than satisfactory political solutions. Nor is there common agreement in the church that the South African regime is illegitimate – requiring it to be rejected. It is this that makes the debate on state illegitimacy, to be considered in the next chapter, a pertinent one in the process of theological and political struggle.

5
State illegitimacy

Armed power can impose a measure of *law and order* in even the most revolutionary situations. It cannot procure *moral legitimacy* from the victims of its aggression. In fact, it could be argued that the moral legitimacy of a regime suffers in direct proportion to the violence employed to maintain law and order. It is this kind of oppression and repression, maintained over a long period of apartheid rule, that has caused an increasing number of people to question the legitimacy of the present South African regime. In the process the depths of the theological heritage of the church are being plumbed for resources on which Christians can draw as they find themselves involved in this legitimacy crisis.

Historical development in the West has predisposed the church to accept the legitimacy of *de facto* rulers, and there are not many occasions in this history when the church has explicitly questioned the legitimacy of any state. Nevertheless, as suggested in a previous chapter, there is a theological tradition in the church which allows that, when a regime becomes *hostis boni communis* (an enemy of the common good) in a persistent way, it is regarded as being no longer 'of God'. As such, it is argued, it can no longer be a servant of the people. In this situation the teaching of the church requires Christians to obey God rather than human authority (Acts 5: 29). This teaching, often disregarded or played-down by the church, is affirmed in the *Kairos Document*.

According to our Christian tradition, based upon what we have already seen in the Bible, once it is established beyond doubt that a particular ruler is a tyrant or that a particular regime is tyrannical, it forfeits the moral right to govern and the people acquire the right to resist and to find the means to protect their own interests against injustice and oppression. In other words a tyrannical regime has no *moral legitimacy*. It may be the *de facto* government and it may even be recognised by other governments and therefore be the *de jure* or legal government. But if it is a tyrannical regime, it is, from a moral and a theological point of view, *illegitimate*.[1]

The *Lusaka Statement*, resulting from a WCC meeting between South African Christians meeting with exiled South Africans and representatives from churches elsewhere in the world, concluded similarly:

It is our belief that civil authority is instituted of God to do good, and that under the biblical imperative all people are obliged to do justice and show special care for the oppressed and the poor. It is this understanding that leaves us with no alternative but to conclude that the South African regime and its colonial domination of Namibia is illegitimate.[2]

While the *Kairos Document* terms the South African government tyrannical, it does not directly state it to be illegitimate. Neither does it deliberately address the complex jurisprudential problem of the relationship between legality and legitimacy, although the implication of the document is that state legality should be grounded in moral and theological principles. The *Lusaka Statement* is less restrained in explicitly declaring the South African regime illegitimate, although it too refrains from deliberately discussing the legal, theological or political implications of this declaration.

The point has already been made that the theology of the church allows political rebellion only in the most extreme situations, while history shows that in practice there have been only a minority of Christians within the church prepared to translate this theology into praxis. It is this in part that accounts for the institutional churches not having investigated the implications of these declarations with any degree of enthusiasm. Some churches have, however, in principle adopted either the *Kairos Document* or the *Lusaka Statement*. Others have in separate resolutions stated that they regard the South African regime to be morally and theologically illegitimate.[3] Should the churches take these resolutions seriously, suggests Frank Chikane, 'the consequences would be far-reaching. The church would then have to take appropriate action in solidarity with others to ensure that the tyrant would be removed from power and a legitimate political authority set up in its place.'[4]

In what follows attention is given to:

1. The identification of a theological tradition within the church, providing theological criteria relevant to the question of illegitimate government. This is essentially what has already been referred to as an *alternative* and minority tradition which co-exists with a

dominant tradition inclined to accept the legitimacy of the existing order. This double theological tradition, it is argued, corresponds to a similar twofold tradition within jurisprudence – seen in the debate between legal positivists and natural lawyers. In defining this double tradition in theology and jurisprudence theoretical attention is given, in slightly more detail, to a theme already referred to in earlier chapters.

2. The political responsibility of theologians and lawyers in crisis situations.

3. A consideration of the distinction between *de facto* and *de jure* rule. In rejecting the dominant tradition which makes *de jure* illegitimacy dependent on *de facto* illegitimacy, an attempt is made to relocate the state legitimacy–illegitimacy debate at the centre of the political process rather than allow it to function as a last resort (cry!) in the face of total political collapse.

A *house divided against itself*

The Christian church has played an ambiguous political role throughout its history. At times it has blessed and legitimated even the most corrupt regimes. At other times groups within the church have rejected existent rulers by affirming the rule of God.

Scholars agree that the origins of the Christian church were of a revolutionary kind. At least for the first three centuries of the common era, the church consisted largely of socially deprived people who were thought by the rulers to be politically subversive. With a strong eschatological belief in the imminent intervention of God into the affairs of humankind, the early Christians saw little need to take their 'pagan' rulers too seriously. This accounted for a certain amount of political indifference but also for their uncompromising obedience to God, with martyrdom regarded as a second baptism and an opportunity to become a perfect imitator of Christ.

But then came the change, giving rise to the *dominant* tradition as we know it within the church today. The Roman empire began to disintegrate, and the character of the church changed as it gained adherents in larger sectors of society, including the army. The Emperor Constantine found it expedient to negotiate with the church, the Edict of Milan followed in 313 C.E. and within a little more than a decade Christianity practically became a state religion. The church was transformed from a persecuted and impoverished social entity into a community of wealth and power. By the high Middle Ages it had become the most despotic political force in

Europe. And when new social and political forces began to reshape the character of Europe, leading to the emergence of the Protestant and Catholic reformations, the control of the church merely shifted from the imperial aristocracy to the bourgeois princes. The peasants, on the other hand, continued to be relegated to a subservient position in the church similar to that which they occupied in the wider social formation. Captive as it was to the dominant forces of what came to be known as 'Western Christian Civilisation', Christianity came to be an important part of the ideological framework that at times quite indiscriminately legitimated the existence of even the most ruthless regimes which claimed to uphold 'Western' and 'Christian' values.

There is, however, also an *alternative* dimension to the Christian tradition. Despite its captivity to dominant or ruling-class ideologies within successive ages, the church never quite managed to deny or suppress a residual revolutionary theology in favour of the poor and the oppressed – traceable back to its earliest history. This is what has already (in accordance with the teaching of Metz) been called a 'dangerous memory' which contradicts the church's social location in society, accounting for marginalised groups within the church being susceptible to revolutionary impulses. It also provides a theological basis for Christians challenging the legitimacy of rulers and the fidelity of laws that violate social justice, good order and the well-being of the people. Gregory Baum has identified the essence of this tradition, in showing that:

… in biblical religion divine transcendence is inextricably linked with holiness and justice. God's majesty makes men tremble not only because God wholly transcends human proportions but because God judges the sinful world, and God's holiness is attractive not only because it offers consolation but because it promises to turn right-side up a world that has been placed upside down by sin.[5]

The alternative tradition, which views rulers and their laws in relation to the majesty and justice of God, necessarily forms the basis of an understanding of church and state different to the dominant tradition, which has shaped society since the Constantinian accommodation.

All religions of radical transcendence allow for the desacralisation of creation, and it is this dimension of the Christian faith, often neglected by the dominant Christian tradition, that the alternative tradition emphasises. It concerns what Max Weber called the pro-

cess of 'disenchantment', within which all human values are shorn
of any claim to ultimate or final significance. For the adherents of
the Christian faith God alone is holy. All creations of humankind –
whether material gain, technological invention or any system of
laws – are necessarily deabsolutised. The sacrosanct, the mysterious
and indeed religious ritual itself are put to the litmus test: that which
is a means of God's grace to us serves the good of humankind and
is worthy of preservation, while that which fails to realise this end
is to be rejected.

The adjacent traditions within Christianity, accounting for two
different theological understandings of the nature of human law
and state legitimacy, have a parallel in a double tradition in jurisprudence. It is a double tradition clearly articulated in the celebrated legal debate of the 1950s between H. L. A. Hart, the Oxford
University-based legal positivist, and Lon L. Fuller, a natural lawyer
and Professor of Jurisprudence at Harvard University.

The *alternative* interpretation of the Christian tradition in fact
raises the same kinds of questions concerning the positivistic tradition within law as those raised by lawyers who stand in the broad
tradition of the natural law approach to jurisprudence in its various
forms.

In arguing that 'law as it is' has an intrinsic worth of its own, Hart
evokes the concern of non-positivistic lawyers and theologians
alike.[6] For him even the death-camp 'laws' of Nazi tyranny (which
he soundly rejects) contained something that rendered them
worthy of being called 'law'.[7] When one enquires as to the nature
of this 'something' that renders even the most hideous forms of
misrule 'law', one discovers that it has something to do with the
'fundamental accepted rules specifying the essential law-making
procedures'.[8] In other words, 'laws', for Hart, are proclamations
which have passed through a given law-making procedure, despite
the possible corrupt or immoral nature of that process. The com-
pulsion to deabsolutise found in radical biblical theology brings it
into direct conflict with positivistic law. 'Law-making procedures'
can never be theologically accepted as self-legitimating. Theologically such procedures must necessarily be demystified.

Interesting, however, is that Hart, despite his positivistic stance,
himself shares in the demystification process, arguing that 'if laws
reached a certain degree of iniquity then there would be a plain
moral obligation to resist them and to withhold obedience'.[9] But
they are still laws! His argument is essentially not only that there is

little to be gained by suggesting that an immoral statute is not a law, but that it is also dangerous to regard it as not being a law – presumably because this could lead to the collapse of a law-governed orderly society. His concern is partly valid. A case can presumably be made for the rule of law in preference to anarchy, even when such rule includes some bad 'laws' and poor government. The question of legitimacy is not, however, raised by such situations, but by situations of *tyranny* or the *persistent violation of the common good*. In these situations Hart's theory of law is not only inadequate (assuming, as it does, a democratic system within which there is equal access to the political arena and a milieu within which moral dissent is taken seriously) but lends itself to abuse in tyrannical situations.

The moral dilemma which emerges from Hart's consideration of immoral law is clearly seen by Lon Fuller. 'On the one hand,' he argues, 'we have an amoral datum called law, which has the peculiar quality of creating a moral duty to obey it. On the other hand, we have a moral duty to do what we think is right and decent. When we are confronted by a statute we believe to be thoroughly evil, we have to choose between two duties.'[10] Fuller's concern is related directly to the kind of concern which emerges in the *Kairos Document*. Here we are reminded that those who wish to change or disobey the unjust and discriminatory laws of apartheid are made 'to feel that they are lawless and disorderly. In other words they are made to feel guilty of sin.'[11] In their very obedience to 'moral duty' they are judged and condemned by the social ethos created by existing laws. The guilt resulting from the violation of these norms predisposes people, with the exception of those of the strongest moral character, to submit to these norms because (as Fuller insists) laws have the 'peculiar quality of creating a moral duty' that they be obeyed. Most people are socialised to believe that law has an intrinsic quality requiring obedience, which means that to call an immoral decree a 'law' goes a long way to ensuring that it should be obeyed.

Some would suggest that this argument has simply to do with nomenclature, with Hart and Fuller ultimately coming to the same conclusion via the use of different terminology. Certain laws, argues Hart, are immoral and therefore need to be disobeyed. Fuller, on the other hand, argues that because certain proclamations fall short of a particular moral standard they are not laws at all and ought not to be obeyed. Language is, however, socially important and Fuller addresses the question concerning the structures of social behaviour with a relevancy for pre-revolutionary times which Hart's theory evades. In pre-revolutionary times, when the social infrastructure has not yet completely collapsed, the question arises whether theologians and lawyers have a contribution to make towards the transforming of society *before* the emergence of a situation of endemic anarchy. This contribution has to do with the creation of a milieu within which people do not simply accept a 'rule of law' and which may even invite revolution as the only alternative to tyranny. The crisis contribution of theologians and lawyers demands the questioning of political obedience. Sometimes it requires civil disobedience, and in extreme cases it necessitates calling into question the legitimacy of the regime as possibly the only alternative to violent revolution.

To fail to recognise the extent to which social symbols, whether these be 'God', the 'free world', 'anti-Communism' or the 'rule of law', shape and manipulate the actions of all but the most determined people of any society is to fail to address the crisis described. Hart argues that it is naive to suggest that it was the Nazi regime's exploitation of subservience to mere law which allowed the horrors of that regime to be perpetrated.[12] It is equally naive to suggest that any mass disobedience to existing immoral 'laws' is possible prior to the disintegration of an existing order (a course of action which Hart would presumably in certain situations justify). Few individuals are prepared to engage (at least while society remains relatively stable) in acts of civil disobedience in the face of laws which morally they would have to concede are, in the words of John Rawls, 'contrary to the sound conscience and sense of justice of all decent human beings'.[13] Churches in South Africa have allowed that it is the theological right and obligation of individuals to disobey laws which conflict with their consciences. Few individuals have, however, seen the need or mustered the courage (at least in more or less 'stable' white areas) consciously to disobey those laws which they judge to be immoral. In black townships, on the other hand, where political disintegration is significantly more advanced, a predisposition to disobey existing laws *is* more prevalent. In such a situation there is a narrow line between disobeying unjust laws and disobeying all law. Ironically the positivist affirmation of law as an end in itself inevitably contributes, in a situation of tyranny, to the collapse of all law.

If law does not (as suggested by Hart) provide its own legitimacy,

what does? Fuller argues that it is the presence of a moral foundation which provides the minimal criteria whereby a decree is worthy
of being called a law. The details of this basic minimum must be
understood politically in terms of social justice negotiated in relation to the demands of a particular society. This is a discussion
beyond the scope of this essay. Fuller's hypothetical question,
however, concerning the drafting of 'a constitution for a country
just emerging from a period of violence and disorder in which any
thread of legal continuity with previous governments has broken',
acquires a certain poignancy for the South African situation.[14] His
question concerns a society within which all dominant values,
customs, traditions, culture and moral appeals have collapsed. In
such a situation law cannot be law simply because it says it is, for the
simple reason that there are no legitimising structures to which
appeal can be made. And when any one political group within that
situation eventually loses either the ability or the will to govern
through the barrel of a gun (if only because there is little left to
govern) the efficacy of law becomes wholly dependent on its acceptance by the people affected by it. Suggests Fuller, 'the provisions of
the constitution should, therefore, be kept simple and under-
standable, not only in language, but also in purpose'.[15]

The complete collapse of the rule of law in South Africa before
the final shot is fired is not unlikely and, as already suggested, to
some extent this situation already prevails in some areas of the
country. In this situation the acceptance of law as inherently legitimate can only decrease, enhancing a dizzy descent into anarchistic
relativism. Fearing this outcome John Dugard encourages lawyers
to be more actively involved 'in the protection of those principles
which make up the country's legal heritage', allowing for the
emergence of 'a new jurisprudential creed to replace legal positivism'. His concern is for a 'value-oriented approach to law, that
recognises the intersection of law and legal values'.[16] This he suggests could get South Africa beyond the present threat to the rule
of law without having to pass through a violent revolution or
Armageddon. What Dugard fails to do is to allow for the kind of
radical discontinuity in values which Fuller speaks of in societies
emerging from politically cataclysmic situations. In such situations
it is the very 'principles which make up the country's legal heritage',
to which Dugard appeals, that are brought into question if not
totally rejected. Sometimes they are rejected because they are
morally corrupt and legally repugnant, and sometimes for no other

reason than that they are part of an oppressive and tyrannical order.

Ronald Dworkin (following Fuller) emphasises the importance of non-formal factors or moral principles as a 'requirement of justice or fairness' in debating the nature and execution of law.[17] He argues that except in the most clear-cut cases, judges invariably 'legislate', exercise discretion and give 'new' content to laws in dealing with cases in court, but not in the unrestrained manner of parliamentary legislators. The discretion and creativity of judges are undertaken in relation to those principles of morality embedded in the existing legal system. As such, legal judgments, for Dworkin, are undertaken in terms of existing moral principles, which means that a particular law cannot simply be ignored because it can be shown to be morally iniquitous. It can be rejected only if it is at variance with the values of the particular legal system of which it is a part. In rejecting legal positivism Dworkin similarly distances himself from classical natural law theory. He does not engage in the radical questioning of the existing order in the way in which Fuller does. He insists that the judge's discretion and interpretative skills can be exercised only in terms of moral principles implicit in and internal to the established legal system.[18] It is this tendency that has persuaded some to argue that Dworkin's theory of law is more positivistic than he is ready to admit. Yet with more restraint than Hart he prefers to argue that it is the task of the judge to 'provide the best constructive interpretation of the community's legal practice'.[19] In other words, he accepts the integrity of the principles underlying the established legal system without offering a serious critique of the system or asking whose interests a particular system may be serving. In South Africa this critique is essential.

The sociological approach to jurisprudence provides an important corrective to universal notions of law and morality. It is a tradition within which law, like any other social ideal or moral imperative, is seen to be the product of social conflict and the struggle for political domination. Whatever the nature of such conflict (and Marxist and non-Marxist sociologists will differ on its exact character), the social-historical source and contextual identity of law are regarded to be hermeneutically as important as its content. Peter Gabel's thoughtful review of Dworkin's *Taking Rights Seriously* makes precisely this point in suggesting that the latter's theory of law is ideologically shaped by a particular socio-economic context, providing legitimacy for what he discerns as an emerging development within capitalism.[20] The values inherent in this socio-economic ideal, no less than any other values of the existing order, are, however, precisely what is called into question by the South African crisis. This suggests that Dworkin and Dugard are insufficiently critical of dominant Western legal values for their theories of law to provide an adequate basis for addressing the credibility crisis that racks political and legal structures in South Africa.

It was argued earlier that two adjacent and intertwined traditions can be identified within the Christian heritage. The dominant theological tradition of the church, captive to existing so-called 'Western Christian Civilisation', is predisposed to a positivistic understanding of law, to be obeyed except in the most extreme situations. South African lawyers are similarly trapped in a legal system which espouses positivism, leaving lawyers and judges, in some instances, required to operate within a system that violates moral conscience. 'I am only doing my job!' is a frequent plea. It is this dilemma that has given rise to the spirited debate between Raymond Wacks and John Dugard on whether judges should resign from the South African bench.[21]

The *alternative* tradition within the church – marginal and appealing to the pre-Constantinian period – weighs all rulers and their laws against the will of God and the fundamental needs of the people. It further affirms a preferential option for the poor and the oppressed (rather than the rich and powerful). As such, it is a 'people's tradition' which recognises that while a government of the people does not necessarily guarantee human justice, justice cannot be obtained without the participation of the people in the political process. Theologians within this tradition find common ground with lawyers whose concern it is to base the legitimacy of rule on a moral deposit located within a rule of law acceptable primarily to those people who are required to bear the brunt of its consequences. It is this community of lawyers and theologians who experience the urgency of the crisis facing the rule of law in South Africa.

The meaning of our time

The New Testament requires Christians to probe the meaning of the time within which they live (Luke 12: 56). Drawing on this tradition, theologians who identify with the *Kairos Document* suggest that this is the time within which 'South Africa has been plunged into a crisis that is shaking the foundations and there is every indication that the crisis has only just begun and that it will deepen and become more threatening in the months to come'. It is a crisis which is a *kairos*, 'the moment of grace and decisive action'. 'It is a dangerous time because, if this opportunity is missed, and allowed to pass by, the loss for the Church, for the Gospel and for all the people of South Africa will be immeasurable'.[22] Some lawyers have, like their theological counterparts, also recognised the urgency of this time, and the emergence of the Democratic Lawyers' Organisation is an important attempt by concerned lawyers to co-ordinate their response to the crisis. More important is the realisation by the overwhelming majority of the people of South Africa not only that the time for change has come, but that change is possible. The agenda of the major Western countries can no longer ignore South Africa, and the southern African sub-continent can know no peace until the South African crisis is addressed. In short, while there are other crisis situations on the world agenda, the *kairos* for South Africa is an idea whose time has come.

This crisis requires that all that society may hitherto have taken for granted be placed under the spotlight of rational enquiry. It is a spotlight which reveals many of the 'laws' which form the basis of the South African legal system to be politically imposed instruments serving the purposes of a small and treacherous minority, and designed to criminalise normal political activity, a process described in Chapter 2.[23] It is this process which, having denied the oppressed black majority virtually every option for non-violent change, has thrust the nation into the initial stages of civil war.

The suffering brought about by this political order has caused its victims to rediscover the liberative theological resources of what has earlier been referred to as the alternative tradition of the church. The consequence is a contextual theology of protest and resistance which obliges the church to address questions of political legitimacy with the kind of urgency that has hitherto been reserved for questions of doctrinal heresy. In so doing, the church immediately recognises that this alternative concern with political affairs as issues of faith is also essentially a *minority* tradition – although one which reaffirms the highwater mark of Christian resistance in modern history, and one that rediscovers the unity of theology and ethical praxis within the early church.

This point is made most clearly in Ulrich Duchrow's important observation concerning the use of the term *status confessionis* (a concept employed by the church to refer to a situation within which the truth of the gospel is at stake). Duchrow shows that not during the Protestant reformation nor at any time since, until Dietrich Bonhoeffer used the term in relation to the 'Jewish question', had it been used in connection with a political question.[24]

Interesting in this regard is the fact that the declaration of the 1982 World Alliance of Reformed Churches (WARC) on apartheid is, in fact, a declaration of heresy against the 'theological justification' of apartheid, although the broader statement which includes the 'heresy' clause does refer to the socio-economic and political implications of apartheid.[25] The Lutheran World Federation (LWF) declaration in Dar-es-Salaam in 1977, on the other hand, in concluding that the situation in southern Africa constitutes a *status confessionis* specifically refers to 'political and social systems' which 'may become so perverted and oppressive that it is consistent with the confession to reject them and work for change.'[26] The *Confession of Faith* adopted by the Nederduitse Gereformeerde Sendingkerk shortly after the WARC heresy declaration also addresses socio-economic and political behaviour in explicit and direct ways.[27]

Suffice it to say that, when theology is written from the perspective of those who suffer most (whether the Jews in Hitler's Germany or blacks in South Africa), it is the alternative tradition of the church which is affirmed. It is this tradition that is today giving rise to the renewal of that part of the church which is located on the side of the poor and oppressed. It is this perspective of theology which also places the alternative church in continuity with the ministry of the poor man of Nazareth, whose concern was primarily with praxis rather than doctrinal exactitudes. 'In the Bible, the atheist [and heretic] is the one who doesn't love. That's who really denies God,' said Fernando Cardenal.[28] In other words, to know God correctly is to do justice. 'Did your father eat and drink and do justice and righteousness,' asked the prophet Jeremiah. 'Then it is well with him. He judged the cause of the poor and the needy. … Is this not to know me? says the Lord.' (Jeremiah 22: 15–16)

J. W. C. Wand argues that the church has traditionally used three criteria in determining whether or not a particular belief or doctrine is heretical. These are criteria with significant implications for praxis as well. A heresy, Wand shows, has traditionally been defined firstly as something completely alien to the broad tradition of the church. The second distinguishing feature has been its partial nature, the affirmation of a part of the Christian tradition to the exclusion of other equally important aspects; and thirdly a heresy has been seen to be a practice pursued with stubbornness, disobedience and persistence.[29] When these criteria are applied to the political structures of the South African state a scenario emerges which corresponds to the heresy situation. Firstly we are obliged to conclude that the prevailing system of law which legalises racial and economic discrimination is a violation of the most fundamental Judeo–Christian values of the tradition within which this system is located. It is a system of laws which violates the affirmation of human dignity which, despite other theological shortcomings, is acknowledged in the Preamble to its own Constitution. And further, what passes for the rule of law in South Africa constitutes a contradiction of the most basic moral values of the West, which it claims to uphold. Secondly, 'law and order' (correctly defined) is an important ingredient of the art of political rule, although one which is absolutised in many states around the world to the neglect of other equally important ingredients of morally legitimate rule. In South Africa, however, 'law and order', defined for the benefit of the few (and enforced by structural and repressive violence), is imposed with a partiality which excludes the most essential human values of Western culture and the ethical centre of the Judeo–Christian tradition. Finally, continual appeals for fundamental change have been continually rejected by the present rulers. It is this that gives credence to the suggestion that 'South Africa is a textbook case of a tyrannical regime hostile to the interests of the majority of the people'.[30] Christians are obliged to oppose such a regime as a matter of faith.

The question of legitimacy

Theologians and lawyers who ply their respective trades within this broad understanding of the moral duty of rulers must be further disturbed when their attention is drawn to the positivistic practice of the courts. And if court proceedings concerning the legal status of Ian Smith's Rhodesian government following the Unilateral Declaration of Independence (UDI) in 1965 are anything to go by, the value-oriented definition of law and state legitimacy is of little significance in the 'real world' of politics, courts and the will to power.[31] The two law-suits which addressed the question of the legal status of the Smith regime both bracketed moral considerations and found *de jure* legitimacy to be a simple corollary to *de facto* control. The problem is that such a finding necessarily minimises the possibility of jurisprudence contributing to the peaceful resolution of major political crises. It also relegates lawyers to sorting out technical distinctions within formal decrees, while the resolution of the crisis is left to those who erect or knock down barricades in the streets.

The court cases involving the legal status of post-UDI Rhodesia hinged on the Kelsenian dictum: 'The principle of legitimacy is restricted by the principle of effectiveness.'[32] The Rhodesian High Court (1968) in the *Madzimbamuto* v. *Lardner-Burke* case found that, although some measure of external sovereignty still resided in the British government, the usurpation of the Rhodesian government was *effective* and seemed likely to continue. In other words, because there was at that time *de facto* control exercised by the Smith regime the court found it to be the *de jure* government of the day. Molteno, commenting on the proceedings, concluded that *if* the Kelsen doctrine of efficacy was applicable in the circumstances, the decision of the court was correct.[33] When the Privy Council heard the case on appeal the outcome was only slightly different. The Council noted that Britain was taking steps to regain control of Rhodesia, and because the outcome of this move could not be predicted, to rule on the status of the usurping government was not yet possible. In a subsequent case, however, involving one Ndhlovu, the Rhodesian Appeal Court interpreted the Privy Court judgment as approving the Kelsen doctrine of efficaciousness and stated that sufficient time had lapsed since the ruling of the Privy Council to rule on Britain's attempts to regain control of the Rhodesian government. The Appeal Court concluded that sanctions were likely to miscarry, and that there was *de facto* control being exercised by the UDI state despite the attempts of Britain to reverse this situation. The Smith regime was, therefore, found to be a *de jure* government.[34]

The rest of the story is well known. The bush war intensified and only when *de facto* chaos prevailed in Rhodesia did Britain and the West conclude that the legitimacy of the Smith regime was in serious question. At horrendous cost the case for the legitimacy versus the illegitimacy of the Smith regime was decided on the battlefield. Having ignored questions of morality in law, the courts also abdicated their political responsibilities in legitimating the Smith regime.

To say that a particular order is legal is to accept the existence of a *de facto* legal system and authority which rules in terms of that system. *Legitimacy*, on the other hand, concerns the criteria for validating the authority to make and execute laws according to a particular legal system. If legitimacy is grounded in nothing other than efficacy, then the rule of law is ultimately the law of the gun. This has major implications for South Africa and many other situations of conflict around the world.

On demystifying government

The democratic process has probably done more than any other form of rule to demystify the nature of government. The pomp, ritual and sacred symbols of liberal democracy (such as 'law and order', the 'rule of law' and the mystification of the legal process) have, however, often sacralised what biblical theology says is not holy and stands in need of desacralising.

Affirming the closest relationship between the will of God and the will of the people without collapsing the one into the other, the Christian tradition allows that it is only when rulers are God's servants that they are able selflessly to serve the good of the people. Romans 13: 4 provides a simple biblical criterion for legitimate rule. The ruler who is to be obeyed, it teaches, is one who is 'God's servant for your good'. Thus the link between love of God and love of neighbour is again affirmed as the heart of the gospel message. A secular document such as the *Freedom Charter*, first adopted at the Congress of the People in 1955 and still today accepted by millions of South Africans as the basis of the democratic struggle in South Africa, in turn, defines state legitimacy solely in relation to the will and good of the people. 'South Africa', it teaches, 'belongs to all who live in it, black and white, and no government can justly claim authority unless it is based on the will of all the people.' It is here that the broad consensus between theology, jurisprudence and politics is found.

The need is for the creation of space within which theologians and lawyers can co-operate in affirming the need for moral legitimacy as a prerequisite for *de jure* rule, rather than allowing the latter to be dependent on *de facto* control. Without consensus on the moral basis of *de jure* rule, the only alternative is the promotion of *de facto* ungovernability, an option with devastating implications.

Theologians and lawyers would do well to reassess the character of even the most democratic nations. With leadership located in the hands of a ruling class whose ideals and advantages are enshrined in a social contract and constitution, nations are slow and reluctant to change. Henry David Thoreau saw this in relation to the United States of America. 'This ... government,' he asked, 'what is it but a tradition, though a recent one, endeavouring to transmit itself unimpaired to posterity, but each instant losing some of its integrity?'[35] The church has a special obligation to pose the legitimacy question in relation to the interests of those who do not benefit from maintaining the status quo.

The process of political change

The appeals of the *Kairos Document* and *Lusaka Statement* are restrained appeals for justice. Accepting that violence is inevitable and refusing to pass moral judgment on those who resort to revolutionary violence in response to the institutional violence of oppression, they affirm the need for an alternative option for change which does not require the promotion of *de facto* chaos. In so doing, the church continues to seek for options of change involving a minimum of violence.

Simply stated, immoral laws tend to undermine *de facto* control and to erode the process of the rule of law. The existence of such laws ultimately leads to revolution. A government may persuade some of the people for some of the time, and it may even persuade itself that *de facto* control through structural and repressive violence can be morally defended as a requirement to ward off the 'communist aggressor' or some other symbol of what is regarded as inherently diabolical. Political reality has, however, a way of ultimately sweeping aside all ideological rationalisations.

An inevitable question follows. If the present rulers in South Africa are not the legitimate leaders of the people, who are? The tried and tested democratic answer is to let the people decide. Political history teaches, however, that tyrants seldom voluntarily surrender to the will of the people. It is this that makes some form of coercive action a required and necessary political instrument in struggle. To a consideration of the role of the church as an instrument of liberation in the coercive process we now turn.

PART THREE

Ecclesial responsibility

6
The church between the times

The horns of resistance and revolution have long been locked in conflict with the horns of oppression and repression in South Africa. This much is clear from the historical analysis in the first part of this book. From time to time the one set of horns has cut deep into the flesh of its opponent, but for the present both jugulars are intact. Some recent events suggest, however, that the sense of 'living between the times' discussed in the Introduction is more pronounced today than at perhaps any time in history.[1]

An important address delivered by Zwelakhe Sisulu on May Day in 1986 makes this point, in response to the decision of a National Education Conference in Durban to recommend that boycotting scholars return to school:

The State has lost the initiative to the people. It is no longer in control of things.

The masses recognise that the moment is decisive and are calling for action.

People are united around a set of fundamental demands and are prepared to take action on these demands.

Having said this, I want to strike a note of caution. It is important that we don't mistake the moment or understand it to be something it is not. We are not poised for the immediate transfer of power to the people. The belief that this is so could lead to serious errors and defeats. *We are, however, poised to enter a phase which could lead to the transfer of power.* What we are seeking to do is to shift the balance of forces in our favour decisively....[2]

A pertinent question concerns the role of the church in this pre-revolutionary interregnum. The identity of the church in this period will determine its role in the actual process of revolutionary change, and its place in the post-revolutionary age. Indeed the church, like the state, is crying out for reform, and theologically Christians need to discover anew what it means to 'live between the times'. In what follows an attempt is made to discover the theological character which the church is obliged to assume in order to meet this challenge.

Where repression and resistance meet

The struggle for the soul of the church occurs at the nexus where repression and resistance meet. It is here, at the very point where children are killed, people enslaved by oppressive ideologies and the poor dispossessed in the name of Christianity and economic development, that hope, fulfilment and a new tomorrow are born.

The dinosaur, suggests Rubem Alves, disappeared not because it was too weak but because it was too strong.[3] Unable to adapt to the changing demands of its environment, it became extinct. The modern totalitarian state, trapped within the 'arrogance of power', feverishly multiplies power upon power on the scale of a global epidemic comparable to a Kierkegaardian sickness that is unto death. With military sophistication and technological near-invincibility the tyrant represses any who dare to question the need or the wisdom of dinosaurian domination of the ecological, economic and political resources of the geographic region within which it is located. Its will to possess and dominate knows no restraint. Totalitarian monsters need total control, both spatial and psychic, in their insatiable hunger for domination. And, like a spoilt child, when the beast senses any danger of losing control it points to the doomsday button which glows with the capacity to end a creation that God declared to be 'very good'. History suggests moreover that the institutional church is in its own way almost as recalcitrant in its refusal to change as the totalitarian state.

Most disturbing is the sense of inevitability with which the beast of domination is allowed to possess the earth and devour its people. Aware of the loss of control over our own destiny and moving ever closer toward an approaching holocaust, too many of us have become conditioned to believe that 'there is nothing we can really do' despite the fact that we are heirs of an Enlightenment era within which women and men had dared 'to be' and 'to do'. Max Weber has likened our condition to existence in a gigantic iron cage where we are held mentally and culturally captive to an all-absorbing, all-controlling bureaucratic organisation that excludes dissident ideas, dysfunctional behaviour and rebellious tendencies.[4] All too often the Orwellian Big Brother or the Ministry of Truth is not even required. Like the characters depicted in Huxley's *Brave New World*, we have come to enjoy our captivity, infatuated by the mechanical orderliness of it all. We are ready to accept the official version of truth, sometimes out of fear and sometimes because there are certain dubious social benefits to be derived from doing so.[5] Within the iron cage of state power, imagination is blunted, hope domesticated and theology is little more than a religious-coated version of a dominant ideology which teaches the oppressed to accept their place in life's socio-economic pile. The malady is advanced in most societies, its victims seduced by their captivity and often unable to recognise or accept healing when it is made available.

The bars of the iron cage are rigid and uncompromising in their captivity of both human body and soul. The Warsaw Ghetto Revolt was the exception rather than the rule as Jews went to Hitler's gas-ovens like sheep to the slaughter. Black South Africans, vastly outnumbering their white oppressors, have not risen in spontaneous revolution. To quote Steve Biko:

All in all the black man [*sic*] has become a shell, a shadow of a man, completely defeated, drowning in his own misery, a slave, an ox bearing the yoke of oppression with sheepish timidity.... The first step therefore is to make the black man come to himself; to pump back life into his empty shell; to infuse him with pride and dignity, to remind him of his complicity in the crime of allowing himself to be misused and therefore letting evil reign in the country of his birth.[6]

The reasons for this 'timidity' are many and complex. Desmond Tutu ascribes it *inter alia* to the education system. 'It is designed', he shows, 'to produce docile unquestioning creatures who could not say "boo" to a goose. They are taught to survive by toeing the line, not rocking the boat and keeping in the herd....'[7] It also has to do with the nature of the white ruling class in South Africa, hellbent on maintaining power through brutal and overt force, but a class which is also sophisticated and well-honed in the powers of political obscuration, confusion and persuasion.

The terrifying strength of the state is possible only because of the comparative weakness of the oppressed. Yet it is within the limitations of this weakness that the hope and power of the poor and the oppressed are to be found.

Differently stated, among those who are forced to the margins of society and there escape the full brunt of social conditioning are found the resources for escaping the iron cage of captivity. The poor discover within themselves and among their own the God of their salvation. They also offer salvation to the comfortable captives of the present age. In other words, it is the poor who are able to evangelise the church. 'Poverty, powerlessness and persecution', suggests Sobrino, 'constitute the real and material conditions for a church in keeping with the will of God.'[8] It is wrong to romanticise poverty. History seems to suggest that abject poverty often leads to social and political debilitation. Nevertheless, history also suggests that the poor, when politically conscientised and empowered by the spirit of liberation (which Christians ascribe to the Spirit of God), can acquire a single-minded commitment against which the iron gates of oppression cannot prevail. This has to do with making a firm and costly choice to be free, a new vision of what is realistically possible and a willingness to translate the most fundamental hopes into heroic praxis.

To this we return later in considering the theological character of the church of the poor. Because this resolve emerges out of a particular history of struggle, however, it is the *reality* of this history (already discussed in Chapters 1 and 2) which must again become a focal point for what follows.

Resistance

Since the earliest days of colonisation repression has been ensured by superior firepower; and the determination and commitment of black youths (which reached a new level of resolve with the 1976 Soweto student revolt) have proved no match for the sophisticated police and military machine of the present white regime. Increased guerilla activity has been effective in heightening white insecurity and has stepped up the cost of security surveillance, but failed to constitute a serious military threat to the South African armed forces.[9]

The oppressed in South Africa have consistently underestimated the extraordinary extent to which the state has been prepared to go in repressing dissent and revolution. Despite the banning of the ANC and PAC in 1960 the forces of resistance remained unprepared for the silencing of virtually every viable black political organisation in the country in October 1976. The shooting, detention and imprisonment of children during the past few years has, in turn, left even hardened activists stunned. And in February 1988 no preparation had been made when the state again defied world opinion and its advocates of reform by restricting seventeen of the most important anti-apartheid organisations inside the country.

The oppressed masses have also experienced internal disruption. Unable to unite across ideological lines, they have been open to real and provoked factionalism. The violence that has always simmered just below the surface among the oppressed classes of any society has been exploited by *agents provocateurs* determined to pit rival groups against one another. The long years of intense oppression in South Africa have caused pent-up aggression and the anger which ought to have been rationally coordinated and directed against the oppressor frequently to manifest themselves instead within the black community. The collapse and disintegration of family and community relations, migratory labour and the systematic suppression of black leadership in the community have all contributed to this process. All this has tended to limit the successes of the resistance movement.

Repression

Over against this history of 'weakness' the state has developed what is the most sophisticated war-machine south of the Sahara.[10] The political influence of the armed forces is clearly a serious factor. Despite certain technological restraints resulting from an international arms boycott (although this is not strictly adhered to) the state's arms production is more than adequate for purposes of internal repression, and the spending habits of the government have each year showed a marked bias in favour of national security.

Most important, however, is the civil–military alliance in South African politics usually referred to under the rubric of the 'militarisation' of culture and society. It is built on the longstanding Afrikaner tradition of martial habits, discipline and obedience to commands.[11] At the same time it has been sophisticated and refined to fit into the structure of the national security state established in Latin America and elsewhere. In recognition of the fact that the outcome of war is decided on the psycho-social plane, every attempt is made through the security apparatus to win the hearts and minds of the people.[12] But if this is not possible, all other means are used to ensure the submission and cooperation of the oppressed – whatever the cost in human rights or life.

F. W. de Klerk, who replaced P. W. Botha in late 1989, has announced the revision of the structures of the National Security Management System (NSMS). This may result in the overt role of the military being constrained. The dominant influence of the police is likely, however, to continue and the structures of political control set up through the NSMS are likely to continue for the foreseeable future.

Instituted initially to coordinate and impose this mechanism of total control, the National Security Management System constitutes the largest and most ambitious attempt ever on the part of the South African state to shape, influence and determine the behaviour, development and thought patterns of the populace.[13] It is South Africa's version of what Comblin has identified as that ideology within which 'national security is the final and unconditional point of reference for everything, the absolute necessity, the unqualified Good; national power is the radical characteristic or nature of all things.'[14] It is a situation in which the state acquires the status of a Leviathan super-organism 'beyond the reach of juridical norms, beyond good and evil'.[15] A frightening possible consequence is found in the words of the former chief of the Argentinian Intelligence Service and later Governor of the province of Buenos Aires, General Saint Jean. 'First we must kill the guerilleros, then collaborators, then sympathizers, then the indifferent and finally the hesitant.'[16]

The origin of the National Security Management System in South Africa can be traced back to the establishment of the State Security Council (SSC) in 1972. A second phase emerged in 1979 with the perceived need to go beyond the collecting of information to the coordination and implementation of government policy. Several functional areas were identified, which included civil defence, culture, government funding, security and transport. Interdepartmental Committees (IDCs) were established to coordinate the work in these areas. The country was divided into twelve regions to coincide approximately with the South African Defence Force's command areas, and Joint Management Centres (JMCs) were created in each of these areas. These in turn were divided into sub-regions and mini-regions and served by sub-JMCs and mini-JMCs, while cities and towns were coordinated by Local Management Committees (LMCs). The third phase of the NSMS emerged after 1980 in response to the revival of resistance politics. In brief the NSMS was used to monitor, respond to and repress what was identified as the 'revolutionary climate' that had emerged. The Interdepartmental Committee for security, renamed the National Joint Management Centre (NJMC), became the *de facto* operational headquarters for dealing with the 'revolutionary climate' that prevailed across the country, and the JMCs, sub-JMCs, mini-JMCs and LMCs were used to coordinate the flow of command down to the grassroots encounter with the people. Almost immediately, individuals serving on these committees (sometimes with well-meaning if naive motives) came to be overtly identified with the repressive and manipulative infrastructure of the government. In brief, the changes proposed by De Klerk to the NSMS concern the structures of the various committees and more especially the JMCs.

The internal structure of the NSMS requires the compulsory participation of government officials and the security forces, but also draws on business, educational, church and other representatives in both direct and, through liaison forums, indirect ways. Ready and able to influence government expenditure and determine which township, area or project receives funding, the NSMS provides an immense incentive to participation in its activities. In brief, via the tried and tested method of carrot and stick, the entire country is monitored and manipulated by the NSMS. Information is obtained on every region, city and township in South Africa, the ideological leanings and persuasions of individual households are monitored, with some regions and individuals being financially and socially upgraded while others are repressed or quite simply destroyed. With military precision and hi-tech management skill resistance and revolution within the country are responded to with force and persuasion, and a 'moderate' and compromised black leadership dependent on government support is being systematically developed as the priority of government 'reform' policy. It remains to be seen to what extent F. W. de Klerk will reform these structures, but it is highly unlikely that the structures of the NSMS are to be dismantled.

This, together with the creation of the Bantustans, a tri-cameral parliament with separate 'coloured' and Indian houses, and the election of black town and regional councillors, has divided the black community against itself. With the assistance of a press bullied into cooperation and the government-controlled media, an appearance of reform and the broadening of democracy are promoted among the unsuspecting and uninformed. When this is linked to the infiltration of organisations of resistance, to the long established police network of spies and informers, to the plethora of laws and to the suspension of the rule of law under successive states of emergency, the extent of state repression is indeed awesome. Many of the structures and processes of repression are showing signs of disintegration, but it is also clear that the white minority regime cannot survive without the continued imposition of repression.

The role of big business, and more especially 'progressive' influences in business vis-à-vis state repression, cannot be dealt with in any detail here. The symbolic visit of leading South African business tycoons to the ANC in Lusaka fuelled speculation that business interests were to use their muscle to break the intransigence of the state. Individual business leaders went further and showed signs of confronting the state but were prevented by business interests from pressing their claims. Such interests are linked to social stability and international trade, and business is obliged to locate itself on a rickety fence – condemning the failures of the regime, while joining the government in coopting a compliant black middle class and pleading forbearance in international trade circles.

'There is widespread acceptance of the need for state intervention to redistribute wealth and address past deprivations,' insists Anglo American's Bobby Godsell. 'All business representatives interviewed for the South Africa Beyond Apartheid project', he tells us, 'accepted that extensive state intervention was not only likely but indeed required in order to create a society of really equal opportunities.'[17] Renfrew Christie, in an otherwise critical review of the study in which Godsell participated, refers to this comment as 'the best statement to emerge from South African business in decades'.[18] To date there is, however, no obvious indication in business circles of an eagerness either themselves to initiate the redistribution process or to persuade the government to do so. 'Eighty years of bold acquisitiveness and political timidity will not be changed overnight.'[19] Having consistently derived benefit from the apartheid system and having defended and financed state policy and repression when required to do so (although sometimes with reluctance), as an institution business remains firmly on the side of South Africa's ruling class. As such, theoretical debate apart, it is *de facto* a partner in state repression.

Where weakness is strength

At one level there is a marked imbalance in the relationship between resistance and repression. At another the determination of those who resist is more pronounced today than perhaps at any other point in the history of political struggle in South Africa. Despite the power of the oppressor, Verwoerd's grand scheme of apartheid has failed. The social, economic, political, psychological and cultural divide between black and white has taken its toll in the creation of a climate of suspicion, hatred and fear. But the dream of a liberated South Africa, free from racism and oppression, continues to inspire not only the oppressed masses but also others of all colours and stations in life to transcend these divisions. (This has something to do with the wise counsel of a Pharisee named Gamaliel who insisted that if something be in accordance with the will of God it cannot ultimately be suppressed or overthrown [Acts 5: 39]. St. Paul spoke of this reality in explaining the relationship between the resurrection and the death and defeat of Christ. 'The foolishness of God', he said, 'is wiser than men; and the weakness of God is stronger than men' [1 Corinthians 1:25].)

Despite the strength of the forces of repression, the signs of vulnerability are more pronounced than ever before:

— International pressure against apartheid is intensifying. Sporting links have been reduced to a mere trickle. More and more international entertainers are shunning lucrative offers to perform on South African stages. The call for economic sanctions is intensifying. The arms embargo is being sorely felt at the level of technologically advanced weaponry, as is evident from the Cuban victory in the battle of Cuito Cuanavale. The United States has already terminated air links with South Africa and several European Economic Community countries have threatened to do the same.

Despite Pretoria's avowal to the contrary, international pressure is producing results. David Beresford, writing in the *Weekly Guardian* in response to an unprecedented international call for the staying of the execution of the Sharpeville Six (sentenced for the alleged involvement in the killing of community councillor Khuzwayo Dlamini in 1984), observed:

When South Africa's Minister of Justice, Mr. Kobie Coetsee, announced the latest indefinite stay of execution for the Sharpeville Six, it represented a rare instance of Pretoria publicly blinking in its confrontation with international opinion.... The country looks more vulnerable than ever before to international pressure.[20]

In November 1988 the State President granted the Six a reprieve. There is a growing realisation inside government and without that South Africa simply cannot survive in international isolation. The response of the state to the hunger-strike by political prisoners and subsequent appeals for the release of political detainees and prisoners which erupted during the first months of 1989 has similarly reflected a reluctance on the part of the state to have these events escalate into a further international embarrassment.

— Economically South Africa is in trouble. A study on economic sanctions included in the transcript of the US Congressional debate on the Anti-Apartheid Amendments Act of 1988 makes a strong case for the effects of sanctions on the South African economy. It reports, *inter alia,* that most respected and sophisticated 'independent' surveys show blacks overwhelmingly endorse the political leadership calling for mandatory comprehensive sanctions and that the government itself concedes sanctions are working. Former South African Reserve Bank Governor Gerhard de Kock was quoted as saying, 'the outflow of capital, the emigration of skilled people [and] the large discount on the financial rand … are all messages that we must heed.… We must first convince the outside world that we are continuing on the road of peaceful and constitutional reform.' The study (included in the Congressional transcript) suggests furthermore that multilateral sanctions would follow if the US shows the will to lead.[21] The report may, of course, not be correct in all its findings, but when read in relation to the Financial Report tabled at the July 1988 meeting of the Commonwealth Committee on Southern Africa, which gives attention to questions of investor self-interest (always a decisive factor), it cannot be ignored. In brief the Commonwealth Report finds that the South African economy is losing the capacity both for internal development and for export growth. In short, South Africa is judged as bad credit.[22]

'Sanctions', says John Kane-Berman, director of the South African Institute of Race Relations, 'could add two million people to the jobless by the year 2000, giving us ten million people without work.'[23] Trust Bank MD Chris van Wyk, in turn, predicts that black unemployment will rise at the rate of 200 000 per year over the next fifteen years at the 'apparent ceiling' of a 2.5 per cent growth rate which present economic conditions allow for.[24] 'I'm fed up with the feeling that we can go it alone, we cannot ignore what sanctions and disinvestment have done,' he said in an interview with the *Wall Street Journal.*[25] A study by Johannesburg Consolidated Investment economist Dr R. Bethlehem, in turn, shows that even partial sanctions will 'ensure a disaster in 12 to 20 years'.[26] Whatever the moral rights or wrongs of sanctions as a means to political change, they mean increased poverty, rising social violence, economic ruin, increasing political instability and the inevitable collapse of social order and the government with it.

— Militarily the South African armed forces are able to deal with current manifestations of internal armed insurgency, but history may need to be rewritten in relation to battles fought before and after Cuito Cuanavale. The ease with which cross-border raids were once conducted by the SADF can no longer be taken for granted. The fighting of surrogate wars through RENAMO, UNITA and other regional fronts will need to be reconsidered. The increased material cost of war will weigh ever more heavily in the wake of an ailing economy. More than that, the possibility of Western governments providing frontline states with defensive missiles and aircraft cannot be ruled out on a permanent basis.[27]

In brief, South Africa's wars are likely to be fought with far less impunity and the cost in lives is likely to increase drastically. South Africa's willingness to negotiate a settlement to the Angolan and Namibian wars is clearly not unrelated to these factors.

Conscientious objection to military service has clearly troubled the state. The End Conscription Campaign (ECC), founded in 1983 as a result of growing support for conscientious objection by white youths, was restricted by ministerial decree in August 1988. Figures differ but indications are that before October 1984 an average of 1 500 conscripts failed to report for duty at each call-up. According to the Minister of Defence this figure rose by 500 per cent in the first call-up after troops were used in the townships. The SADF subsequently announced that this figure was 'incorrect' but declined to release figures for subsequent call-ups, although court cases and SADF sources indicate that attendance at army camps is generally between 40 per cent and 60 per cent.[28] The Minister of Defence saw fit to name the ECC together with the ANC, UDF and the South African Communist Party as one of four of the most dangerous organisations in South Africa.[29]

— Internal pressure has reached an all-time high. The fact that South Africa is presently enduring its second successive state of emergency is indicative of the level of internal resistance to apartheid. The strength to be discerned in the weakness of resistance in South Africa (which includes school boycotts; children trying to keep armoured-cars, Casspirs and Buffels at bay with sticks and stones; women standing up for their rights; trade union activities; and guerilla strikes) is that it evokes the international responses already discussed. And there is no sign that it will abate.

The interregnum continues. South Africa is locked into living between the times. Clinging to the last vestiges of power, the state can exact a high price for the liberation of the oppressed. But when, for example, demographic realities and an already splintered white ruling-class response to internal and external pressure are considered in addition to the above, it is clear that the inevitable cannot be indefinitely delayed. The question concerns the role of the church in this situation.

Towards a new way of being the church

'By kindness,' it has been suggested, 'Constantine achieved what his predecessors had not been able to achieve by force. Without a threat or a blow, and all unsuspecting, the Christians were led into captivity and their religion transformed into a new imperial cult.'[30] Whatever the motive – and it was probably what Machiavelli called *virtu* rather than 'kindness' – the outcome was the emergence of a new alliance between church and state founded on religious opportunism and political expediency.

The church in South Africa has since its earliest missionary days shared in the subjugation of the masses. The Afrikaans Reformed Churches shared in the creation of a rigid ideology of racial and economic exploitation and oppression. The mission activity of the English-speaking churches, in turn, destroyed the social structure of African society and, after the discovery of gold in 1886, the church found itself located firmly on the side of the dominant forces of white supremacy and capitalist exploitation.[31] The historic and indigenous black churches have in most instances modelled their self-identity on the political acquiescence of the dominant churches – or alternatively provided an escape from political responsibility through the promotion of ecstatic religious experience. This is, however, a history which is by no means unique to the South African context. It is a history with parallels around the world, where churches have spawned generations of conquistadors and plunderers.

The church has nevertheless also given rise to people of God who have in the most adverse situations sought to proclaim the liberating gospel of Jesus Christ. The self-contradiction of dominant church and (for the rich and powerful) its Achilles heel is the presence of the poor within this church, whose cries of oppression have been heard by generations of turbulent priests, recalcitrant prophets and dissident members. Through the cries, pain and suffering of the poor, the church has always been disturbed and challenged. In recent times it has been forced to rediscover its earliest identity in the poor man of Nazareth who turned away from a religious establishment that was prepared to cooperate with the dominant political and economic forces of the time. What is perceived to be a 'new way' of being the church is in reality a return to Christianity's most heroic and appealing origins. And yet, now as then, this relocation appeals more to some than to others; now as then, it is the poor who hear the message of Jesus gladly while the rich turn sorrowfully away (Mark 10: 22).

The character of the alternative church is formed by a *theologia viatorum* or a pilgrim theology. By definition it must strike tents and never settle for a fixed existence – glorifying neither any past nor any present manifestation of ecclesial identity. This church is necessarily in continual reformation, sharing in what Paul Lehmann has called God's 'permanent revolution'.[32] Theologically it can afford only one permanent ally, in the poor and oppressed of each successive age, and this means that in effect its alliances may change from one generation to the next.

A concrete programme of action for the church in solidarity with the poor and the oppressed (indeed *for* the church of the poor and oppressed) within the present South African context, is presently being grappled with and formulated by many Christians within and outside the institutional churches. Old forms of protest and resistance are simply no longer adequate. James Cochrane makes the point well: 'What was understood as "resistance" once may no longer appear as anything other than anachronistic activity now, or at the least, as something far less than is demanded by new circumstances.'[33] No attempt is made in what follows to propose a concrete strategy of resistance. Rather, a theological framework is proposed within which such strategies can be defined.

The enduring theological features which distinguish the alternative church from what has emerged as the dominant church are essentially three: it reaches beyond social neutrality, it affirms a position beyond bourgeois realism and it promotes an ethic which takes it beyond moral appeal. To a consideration of these features we turn.

Beyond political neutrality

It is almost trite to point out that the church has never hesitated to take sides. Constantine snatched the imperial crown from his rivals, inspired, says Eusebius of Caesarea, by the appearance of the cross of Christ in the heavens; and the church soon honoured him as the 'friend of God'. Medieval Europe was conquered in the name of Christ. The Protestant Reformation was as much a struggle for national independence built on Christian identity as a movement of religious reform. Columbus colonised the new world bearing the sword and the cross, Cortes conquered the Aztecs and the Mayas, and Pizarro with his conquistadors, blessed by the Spanish alliance of church and state, slaughtered the Incas and other native peoples in Peru and elsewhere. Kaiser Wilhelm's troops crawled out of their besieged bunkers, buttons embossed with the words '*Gott mit Uns*'. The amalgam of Christian and cultural symbols in the USA has produced coins celebrating that nation's trust in God. In British colonies soldiers died 'for God, Queen and country'. Afrikaner nationalists, in turn, have used the Bible to legitimate an ideology of oppression in a way so obvious that Christians around the globe have been obliged to cry, 'heresy!'

Such abuses of the Christian faith have caused some to insist, 'never again', and use this as an excuse to oppose contextual and liberation theologies which promote the cause of the poor and oppressed against the privileges of the rich and the powerful. The recent shift by the South African state regarding the social function of religion is located precisely here. Until very recently state pronouncements had encouraged the synthesis of religion and politics which lies at the heart of traditional Afrikaner nationalism, and vigorously defended white patriotic theology.[34] But then came the legitimation crisis. Verwoerdian notions of whites having been planted on the southern tip of Africa by divine intent in order to provide guardianship for blacks had become a political embarrassment. This persuaded the white NGK to rewrite its theological basis for human relations, substituting its earlier 'hard' biblical support for apartheid with a 'softer' and more nuanced acceptance of government policy.[35] The structural inability of the NGK categorically to reject apartheid has, however, again been reinforced at the Vereeniging consultation between representatives of the black and white churches of the NGK family of churches.[36]

The problem is that while its own theological legitimation had been undermined, the liberatory themes of the biblical and theological tradition had been claimed by the oppressed of South Africa and elsewhere in the world with a measure of acceptance that Afrikaner theology had never achieved. In this milieu the 1983 Eloff Commission of Inquiry into the South African Council of Churches had only one reasonable option at its disposal and it grabbed at this: All 'political theology', it said, whether 'for the state' or 'against the state', was to be rejected.[37] The shift in official state policy was

towards a classic secularist position on religion. Noting the prolif-
eration of conflicting religious views and recognising that there
could be no definite religious answers to complex religious prob-
lems, the Commission decided that the solution was for churches
to refrain from involving themselves in politics at all. The Commissioner of Police, who gave evidence before the Commission, insisted that the churches should stick to matters of 'personal
salvation and conversion'. The official Eloff Report, in turn, concluded that the true gospel addresses 'only truly spiritual purposes',
and that politics are best left to the secular forces of 'national
interest'.[38] What had hitherto been the national task of the patriotic
churches had now become the concern of the national security
apparatus of the state.

Within the context of the national security system, right-wing
religious groups which hail the South African state as a bastion
against all manner of 'godless' ideologies have a key role to play.
They are courted, encouraged and facilitated by the state, and the
state-supported military chaplaincy continues to endeavour to persuade its recruits of the sanctity of the apartheid war. But officially
the theological legitimation of white conquest is no longer openly
promoted by the state. In its place a new, more subtle and more
dangerous form of theological subterfuge has emerged, which
enjoys support well beyond the confines of the pro-government
NGK. It comes in the form of a plea that oppressed people be not
allowed to fall into the kind of theological trap that others have
fallen into before them.

Vigilance in politics is always a good thing and the church has a
special responsibility in this regard, but before addressing this
concern it is necessary fully to understand the deception of the
theological solution suggested.

This solution is well documented in J. A. Loubser's *The Apartheid
Bible: A Critical Review of Racial Theology in South Africa*.[39] Apartheid
theology, Loubser tells us, began as a people's theology and came
into its own in promoting the cause of the Afrikaner, lured to the
cities by the industrialisation process during the early part of the
century. As such, he says, it showed 'amazing similarity' with the
concern for the poor and oppressed found in the NG Sending-
kerk's *Confession of Faith* and the *Kairos Document*. The problem,
according to Loubser, is that theologies like Afrikaner apartheid
theology are written explicitly and self-consciously in response to
particular experiences of human suffering. According to Loubser,

this is where both liberation and apartheid theologies go wrong. It is therefore logical, he thinks, that in rejecting apartheid theology we also reject all contextual and liberation theologies. And the answer? It is, he suggests, beyond both apartheid theology and *kairos* theology – a 'third option' theology.

Apartheid theology has, of course, never been identical with (or shown 'amazing similarity' to) liberation theology as we know it today. The former has always promoted the exclusive, chauvinistic, oppressive and partisan cause of whites and more explicitly Afri-kaner whites, to the exclusion of the infinitely poorer black masses. Not by the furthest stretch of the imagination is this partisan or racist dimension included in liberation theology of any kind, and certainly not in either the *Kairos Document* or the N.G. Sending-kerk's *Confession of Faith*.

'Third option' theology has, however, gained in currency also in other circles, as the theological pendulum has swung increasingly in the direction of the oppressed in the South African context. The Doctrine Commission of the Methodist Church of Southern Africa, for example, warned against what it perceived as a tendency in the *Kairos Document* 'to absolutise the evil and the good of opposing forces', thus implying that within the present crisis 'there are only two options – support for apartheid or for the strategy of peoples' organisations'. 'This', says the Methodist response, 'we do not accept.' Opting for a classical 'third option' position, the Methodist Church proposed that 'the church must continue its search for a mode of action appropriate to its subjection to the Word of God', without stating what this would involve by way of a programme of action.[40] The closest it came to doing so was in a subsequent report written by an official Methodist study-group, which proposed that the Methodist Church become a 'Peace Church' and reject 'all forms of violence'. Intended to allow the Methodist Church for-mally to support conscientious objectors to military service, ironi-cally this report stated that such a decision should not be con-fessionally binding and that individuals were free to decide whether or not to serve in the South African armed forces. The church was not prepared to resist the South African military machine and certainly not prepared to accept the legitimacy of an armed struggle by guerilla forces. It was this vacillation that resulted in the proposal being voted down in the courts of the church, with constituencies to the 'left' and the 'right' opposing this kind of 'third way' theology.[41]

Yet, perhaps it is Walter Wink's book entitled *Jesus' Third Way* that has done most to popularise 'third option' theology in South Africa.[42] Whatever his intentions (and they were not to support the non-action of the liberal churches), in situations of high-level conflict the implication of 'third way' language is that the Christian option is somehow located equi-distant between the oppressor and the oppressed. In reality 'third options' simply do not substantively exist in South Africa. More important, however, is the fact that the liberative message of the Scriptures protects the poor and the oppressed, historically the victims of expropriation, compromise and extortion, from settling for anything less than their undeniable right to be free – and in South Africa that translates as one-person-one-vote in a unitary state.

The gospel can never be reduced to a particular political ideology, but neither can it ever be used as an excuse for Christians not to participate in an actual revolution. The church can never be synonymous with a particular liberation movement, but it is theologically obliged to share in the liberation process. Karl Barth's theological response to revolutionary change remains of cardinal importance for theo-political debate. He showed undeniable bourgeois hesitation about revolution when, in his *Epistle to the Romans*, he warned 'that the revolutionary Titan is far more godless, far more dangerous than his reactionary counterpart', but he was theologically and morally clear enough to insist that this was 'because he [the revolutionary] is so much nearer the truth'.[43] One recalls with interest that Gollwitzer once suggested that Barth's social and academic station in life prevented his theology from realising its full 'anti-bourgeois' potential![44] Barth insisted that the revolutionary was wrong despite the wrongness of the reactionary – but wrong primarily, as he states in the second edition of the *Epistle to the Romans*, because God's grace requires 'impatience, discontent, dissatisfaction…. [It] is the enemy of even the most indispensable "interim ethic."'[45] For Barth the most responsible theological participation in the political arena required a 'God-given restlessness' and 'critical opposition to life' in pursuit of the 'revolution which is before all revolutions', that revolution which implied for him the restoration of God's creation in the present situation.[46] The gospel, as the source of God's revolution, is always more demanding and more radical than any solution humankind can offer. God's revolution, suggests Paul Lehmann, enables the human revolution 'to be and to stay human in the world'. It also prevents the revolution 'from devouring its own children'.[47]

And yet even this theology of 'permanent revolution' has been appropriated and used by some (as the history of Barthian ortho- doxy has shown) as an excuse not to engage actively in the actual struggle for justice. In order to avoid this most sanctimonious and (by implication) politically reactionary attitude to life it is import- ant to discern what Horkheimer has called the 'theological mo- ment' in politics.[48] This concerns not only a need to ensure the continuing critique of all political options, but also the identifica- tion of that moment in history when the possibility of radical social change for the better is possible. Differently put, it concerns the *kairos*, 'the moment of grace and opportunity, the favourable time in which God issues a challenge to decisive action'.[49] This requires us, in the words of Barth, to acknowledge that 'we do not really know Jesus if we do not know him as this poor man, as this partisan of the poor and finally as this revolutionary'.[50]

There is only one way in which the church is theologically required to be totally impartial, favouring neither the poor nor the rich, neither the oppressed nor the oppressor, and that concerns its obligation to preach the gospel to all people. The gospel may favour the cause of the poor but the church dare not choose to whom it shall preach that gospel. The gospel may be heard gladly by the poor or even rejected by the rich, but it is a message for both the poor and the rich. But to preach that gospel is, by implication, a case of taking sides for the simple reason that it involves the empowering of the poor.

Beyond bourgeois realism

The gospel is also a message for the one who proclaims it, requiring her, him or the church as community to affirm and promote the vision and the goals of the gospel. Bluntly put, there is no room in the alternative church for bourgeois notions of realism. Yet neither is the cause of justice served by what has been called romantic 'Pollyanna-ish' or 'heaven on earth' idealism.[51]

Reflecting on the 'Perils of American Power' in 1932, Reinhold Niebuhr thought the United States to be 'the most powerful and most ignorant of all nations' and resisted attempts to provide it with military power equal to its economic power.[52] But, with the debate having been overtaken by history as a result of the United States having entered World War Two, he came to accept and legitimate the power of the United States in global politics.[53] In so doing he insisted on a brand of Christian social realism that allowed for the competing interests of all concerned, a realism that allowed for what Niebuhr called 'calculated' situations of compromise. This resulted in his accusing Barth of 'eschatological irresponsibility'. This was not, however, because of Barth's affirmation of the uncompromising ethic of the revolution of God, but (ironically) because Barth had 'realistically' (from the perspective of a conquered people) counselled the Hungarian Reformed Church to seek areas of cooperation with the Communist authorities. (Niebuhr thought Barth had adopted a dangerous 'neutralist' position in the East–West Cold War, while Barth regarded Niebuhr as having allowed himself to become a spokesperson for the anti-Communist crusade of the West – which he insisted was more dangerous than Communism itself.) [54]

In brief Niebuhr's notion of Christian realism begs the question: realism according to whom? Paul Tillich's perceptive essay entitled 'Reinhold Niebuhr's Doctrine of Knowledge' has a nice opening sentence: 'The difficulty of writing about Niebuhr's epistemology', he writes, 'lies in the fact that there is no such epistemology. Niebuhr does not ask, "How can I know?"; he starts knowing.' [55] Bluntly put, having failed to exercise the necessary epistemological vigilance, Niebuhr's teaching on social realism falls captive to First World, West-centred ways of viewing reality. Summarily, Niebuhr's sense of reality shows signs of what John Coleman has called 'imperialistic realism'. [56] Beverley Wildung Harrison and other feminist theologians, in turn, legitimately censure Niebuhr for his male-dominated understanding of reality, although this can presumably be said of most male theologians of his and the present generation. [57]

A church in an age of revolution has a special obligation to reach beyond bourgeois or 'existing' notions of realism. What are perceived as realistic compromises by the power centres of the world or of society are often not what constitutes the realism of the poor and the oppressed, or of women. Niebuhr's politically chastened realism is an antidote to romantic idealism, but it also carries within it the danger of complacency; this may kill a faith that anticipates the destruction of that reality which oppresses the poor and represses those who seek to liberate themselves from its 'inevitability'.

Revolutions seek to change political, economic, cultural and mental constructions of reality. Such acts, suggests Alves, 'must necessarily be considered absurd, insane, irresponsible, heretical or subversive by the Organisation it proposes to supersede'.[58] Those whose very existence is not threatened by existing reality have no cause to dream new, 'irresponsible' and subversive dreams. Vision, hope, imagination and creativity are born of suffering and pain. That is partly why Karl Marx identified the proletariat as the only truly revolutionary class – they have nothing to lose except their chains in translating dreams into reality. From our perspective, more telling is the biblical emphasis on those who are marginalised from the all-imposing dominant notions of what is most real, inevitable and irrevocable. It is the revolutionary poor and oppressed, of each successive age, those who have no obvious reason to hope, who are compelled to hope. They are often regarded by bourgeois realists as romantics, fools and cannon-fodder when they are able to reject the dominant notions of reality. Yet within this rejection often resides a latent but Promethean sense of human determination. Perhaps it is only from within situations of desperation that the most creative history-making events emerge. Bonhoeffer spoke of this kind of human determination and commitment when he reflected on the mood of those who conspired to kill Hitler in the dark days of the early 1940s:

Surely there has never been a generation in the course of human history with so little ground under their feet as our own. Every conceivable alternative seems equally intolerable. We try to escape from the present by looking entirely to the past or the future for our inspiration, and yet without indulging in fanciful dreams, we are able to wait for the success of our cause in quietness and confidence. It may be however that the responsible thinking people of earlier generations who stood at a turning point of history felt just as we do, for the very reason that something new was being born which was not discernible in the alternatives of the present.[59]

The 'uniqueness' of the German experience was in a sense the uniqueness of each successive organic crisis in history. The quest in such situations is necessarily for what is indeed new and what is not discernible in the present (realistic) alternatives. And, in turning away from fanciful dreams and showing the necessary quietness and confidence of the hour, the quest manifests itself (as was the case with Bonhoeffer) in radical action. It is a situation in which oppressed people are compelled to seek for new perceptions of what is possible, and the urgency of their need obliges them to discern viable ways of realising this new reality in history. Karl Rahner is correct: 'The Church can be wide off the mark in such [practical] imperatives and directives' and 'more palpably so than in theoretical declarations'. 'But this', he warns, ' is a risk that must be taken if the Church is not to seem to be pedantic, to be living in a world of pure theory, remote from life, making pronouncements that do not touch the stubborn concreteness of real life.'[60] If others in situations of crisis are obliged to act with no guarantee of having made the correct decision, the church cannot afford the luxury of avoiding such risk.

The church's special responsibility in a revolutionary situation is to relate such perceptions, dreams and actions to the biblical record of earlier generations of oppressed people of God. This must never, however, be a blind and uncritical legitimation of revolution. Christians have a God-given task to ensure that all revolutionary action is directed towards what has already been referred to as 'the revolution before all revolutions' – a revolution given in creation and fulfilled in eschatology, which provides a mythical notion of God's purpose for God's world. The church has a responsibility to empower the poor and the oppressed to ensure that the revolution remains their revolution. It must not play into the hands of oppressors who seek to reinforce notions of impotency among the poor. Neither must it allow others to use the revolution for their own ends and against the poor.

Central to this process of empowerment is the need for the church to rediscover the importance and place of worship in revolution. It concerns the reintegrating of liturgy into the experiences of everyday life. The Eastern Orthodox understanding of 'two inseparable movements' which gather together the people of God and send them into the world as a single 'rhythm of mission' is an alien notion in the church of the West.[61] For theological empowerment to occur within a revolutionary culture, the church is obliged to rediscover the integration of the 'sacred' and the 'secular' in worship, to relearn that worship (properly related to life) is the chief end of humankind.

Places of worship need to become centres of alternative cultural renewal, and liturgy a source of imagination and anticipation of a new and transformed spiritual, mental and social sense of reality. The American poet Wallace Stevens has suggested that in true worship we encounter 'a reality that forces itself upon our consciousness and refuses to be managed and mastered'.[62] If worship is to be an encounter with God as Ultimate Reality, it is this Reality which needs to shape our perceptions of social reality. We dare not, as Christians, allow our striving, our goals and our action to be shaped and determined by bourgeois notions of what is possible. To do so is to ignore the eschatological vision of the Bible that acts as an indispensable antidote to all forms of political oppression in society.

It could be that the single most important service which the church can render the poor is to provide an alternative vision of what by God's grace is socially possible. The church has a theological obligation to counter the imperious sense of inevitability and social reality which the oppressors impose on the oppressed. In order to do so the church must itself hear the voice of the poor and the oppressed who resist this oppression and strive in hope for a sense of social reality grounded in justice and peace, and must itself proclaim it from the rooftops.

It is the task of the church to infuse what is qualitatively new (a new sense of what is historically possible) into human reality. It is this which constitutes the essence of the gospel.

Beyond moral protest

It is, however, insufficient for this word of resistance and hope to be affirmed merely in a conceptual or spoken manner.

The history of churches opposed to apartheid is a history of moral outrage. Every new wave of repression has been protested against, and ecclesial records document the sense of moral exasperation with which the English-speaking churches, Roman Catholics and others have responded to apartheid. Reluctant, however, to translate their moral concern into viable programmes of resistance, the institutional churches have failed to stem the tide of intensified repression. They have also opposed the more radical forms of protest and resistance perpetrated by some secular groups, and often shunned the opportunity themselves to move beyond theological critique to actual participation in the struggle for liberation.

In so doing the churches have deviated from the biblical understanding of truth which is emphatically more than principled or theoretical truth. In the biblical tradition truth is not *gnosis*, but a way of living or acting in obedience to God's creative and redemptive participation in human history. It is a history-making activity. The Convocation of Churches which met in Johannesburg in May 1988 acknowledged the failure of the churches to give expression to truth in a pro-active biblical way in their moral protest over the years, and committed themselves to translate their moral abhorrence of apartheid into a programme of non-violent direct action.

This constitutes a new emphasis in the life of the churches in South Africa. They are not historically well-equipped to cope with the new responsibility which they have taken on themselves. It remains, in fact, to be seen whether this commitment to action can become an institutional reality, and how the churches will respond to the demands which the revolutionary poor make of them now that virtually all other structures of opposition to state control and repression have been closed down by state decree. Important in this regard is whether the church can and will respond theologically and as church to these demands.

The institutional church may well refuse to allow itself simply to be used by activists whose secular organisations have been banned and now (often with a measure of scepticism) seek its hospitality and support. There are, however, some within the church who, being aware of their own lack of the adequate ecclesial resources of resistance, abdicate responsibility to 'secular' activists better equipped to cope with the present crisis. For the church, however, to be the church in a revolutionary situation, it is required to rediscover theological and moral resources that enable it to share in the liberation struggle. And ultimately it is this rediscovery of its own true revolutionary identity (as already discussed) that constitutes the major contribution of the church to the present age.

The quest, however, for theological and moral resources occurs within what is frequently an indifferent if not hostile environment. But this environment is partly of the church's own making. Theological statements and moral outrage have in the past often constituted a substitute for resistance, and this has contributed to a serious distrust of moral discourse in any sense.[63]

Machiavelli's determination to locate politics beyond morality has produced a legacy of converts to the 'left' and 'right' of the political divide. History confirms that self-interest and power are the essential ingredients in any cauldron of change. The successful process of political change beneficial to the poor and oppressed has nevertheless inherent in it a sense of moral value – and ultimately it is only this revolution (where morality and politics meet) which can be theologically defended or supported as a cautious step towards God's revolution.

The task of the church in a revolutionary age is then quite simply theologically and morally to generate a climate of activity or praxis which manifests itself in a series of bold history-making interventions against oppression and for the liberation struggle. Its special task as church is, however, to ensure that this struggle and revolution ultimately serves the poor. Again, only this revolution can be part of the continuing revolution of God.

The moral outrage and theological affirmation which functions as the cause, instigator and motor of a culture of resistance and restless renewal rejects moral indignation which stops short of liberatory praxis. As praxis, it also resists the influences of power and self-interest which turn politics into a contest for domination. It is an exercise in transforming moral power and theological claims, in solidarity with the poor, into political process.

Such power is seen in the heroic refusal of people to vacate their traditional homes under the threat of Group Areas removals. It is seen in the struggles through which migrant labourers and their families refuse to be separated by pass laws and influx control. It is seen in the refusal of children to accept an inferior and repressive education. It is seen in youths who will go to prison rather than accept another generation of apartheid. It is seen in the refusal of white youths to serve in the South African armed forces. It is seen when Christians, under the threat of imprisonment, call for non-participation in apartheid structures and compromised elections. It is seen in the action of Nelson Mandela who refused to accept conditional release from prison. It is seen in the resort to armed struggle of those people who feel that all other options of resistance have been exhausted. It is seen in the tears of a mother who refuses to be intimidated by a policeman who has shot her child. It is seen in the suffering of those who languish in resettlement camps. Their relentless hope and fervent prayer constitute a form of silent resistance in which they anticipate the day when their daughters and sons shall be free in the land of their birth.

When moral outrage and theological confession are manifest in such actions, they represent a form of political power against which military might and state repression are quite simply inadequate. The church which not only affirms the right of the poor and oppressed to be free but empowers them in their quest is a church which the most radical revolutionary cannot afford to ignore. It brings, suggests Paul Lehmann, the power of weakness into direct confrontation with the weakness of power.[64] It is this that purifies the revolution from within.

The shape of the church to come

The struggle for the possession of religious symbols, theological traditions and religious identity is being fiercely contested between the forces of renewal and the forces of reaction in South Africa. This has given rise to two increasingly distinct churches, an alternative and a dominant church, discernible within the institutional churches. It is too early as yet to judge which will prevail.

It could be that the ecumenical church of the future is presently being born within this conflict and in similar conflicts elsewhere in the world – in Nicaragua, the Philippines, Guatemala, Chile, Brazil, and the Middle East. Here too the identity of the traditional church is being challenged by a church in resistance, a church of the poor, the people's church. It is a church which insists that the good news of Jesus should have liberatory significance in the most concrete forms of captivity in the streets of Managua, Manila, Guatemala, Santiago, Sao Paulo, Beirut and Soweto, failing which it is not good news at all. As the church of the two-thirds world impinges more acutely on the First World church it could be that the global church will undergo a reformation as drastic as any it has undergone during the past two thousand years.

But, as in earlier times of ecclesial transition, the result may well be a radical schism between reactionary and change-oriented forces within the church. Perhaps, also, those committed to the significance of the gospel for socio-economic and political crises at present most obviously manifest in the peripheral areas of the globe (but which must in time reach into Washington, London, Bonn and other 'centres' of the West) will simply look elsewhere for institutions through which to strive for a more just, more sustainable, more participatory and more human society. The church will then be reduced to the restricted and exclusive area of private concern – a kind of club for internal migration and spiritual introspection. It will be thrust into the margins of history. Alternatively it could be forced into exile where renewal may be thrust upon it.

References

Introduction

1. Quoted in Leonardo and Clodovis Boff, *Introducing Liberation Theology* (Tunbridge Wells, Kent: Burns and Oates, 1987), p. 25.

2. *Ibid.*

3. Antonio Gramsci, *Selections from the Prison Notebooks*, edited by Q. Hoare (London: G. Nowell Smith, 1971), p. 276.

4. In a conversation with the author in Hamburg in 1979.

5. C. Villa-Vicencio, *Between Christ and Caesar: Classic and Contemporary Texts on Church and State* (Grand Rapids: Eerdmans. Cape Town: David Philip, 1986).

6. J. B. Metz, *Faith in History and Society: Towards a Practical Fundamental Theology* (London: Burns and Oates, 1980), pp. 88f.

7. Shula Marks, 'The Ambiguities of Dependence: John L. Dube of Natal', *Journal of Southern African Studies*, 1, 2, 1975, pp. 162–180.

8. Shula Marks, 'Khoisan Resistance to the Dutch in the Seventeenth and Eighteenth Centuries', *Journal of African History*, 13, 1, 1972, pp. 55–80.

9. Quoted in Boris Nicolaievsky and Otto Maenchen-Helfen, *Karl Marx: Man and Fighter* (Harmondsworth: Penguin Books, 1983), p. 398.

10. Fatima Meer, 'African Nationalism: Some Inhibiting Factors', in Heribert Adam (ed.), *South Africa: Sociological Perspectives* (London: Oxford University Press, 1971), p. 150.

11. Quoted in Robert Edgar, *Because They Chose the Plan of God: The Story of the Bulhoek Massacre* (Johannesburg: Ravan Press, 1988), p. 36.

12. See discussion in Robert Ross, *Cape of Torments: Slavery and Resistance in South Africa* (London: Routledge and Kegan Paul, 1983), p. 9.

13. Reinhold Niebuhr, *The Nature and Destiny of Man*, 1: *Human Nature* (New York: Scribner's Sons, 1964), p. 181.

14. Walter Wink, *Violence and Nonviolence in South Africa: Jesus' Third Way* (Philadelphia: New Society Publishers, 1987), p. 43.

15. W. Beinart and C. Bundy, *Hidden Struggles in Rural South Africa*

(Johannesburg: Ravan Press, 1987), p. 40.

16. K. Marx and F. Engels, 'The Eighteenth Brumaire of Louis Bonaparte', in *Selected Works* (Moscow: Progress Press, 1968), p. 95.

17. Karl Barth, *The Epistle to the Romans* (London: Oxford University Press, 1960), p. 430.

18. Karl Barth, *Church Dogmatics* (Edinburgh: T. & T. Clark, 1956), IV/I, p. 121.

19. Contained in the report of the South African Council of Churches, *God's Project of Humanising the World: Documentation about the Visit of the SACC Delegation to the Middle East Council of Churches.* Unpublished.

20. In this regard, I acknowledge James Cochrane's important response to my paper 'Law, Theology and Civil Disobedience', read at the South African Theological Society meeting in Stellenbosch in 1988.

21. See Chapter 6, for a discussion on the national security state.

22. Friedrich Nietzsche, *Thus Spake Zarathustra*, VI.

23. Karl Barth, *The Epistle to the Romans*, p. 43.

1 Early resistance

1. E. P. Thompson, *The Poverty of Theory and Other Essays* (London: Merlin Publishers, 1978), pp. 345–6.

2. Greg Cuthbertson quoting Gladwin and Saidin, *Slaves of the White Myth*, in 'The English-Speaking Churches, Colonialism and War' in *The Theology of Violence: The South African Debate*, ed. C. Villa-Vicencio (Johannesburg: Skotaville Press, 1987), p. 17.

3. Marks, 'Khoisan Resistance', p. 70.

4. Major R. Ravan-Hart, *Before Van Riebeeck* (Cape Town: C. Struik, 1967), pp. 1–11; Richard Elphick, *Kraal and Castle: Khoikhoi and the Founding of White South Africa* (New Haven and London: Yale University Press, 1977), pp. 71–89.

5. Elphick, *Kraal and Castle*, p. 82.

6. Henry Bredenkamp and Susie Newton-King, 'The Subjugation of the Khoisan during the 17th and 18th Centuries', p. 4. A paper delivered at the Conference on Economic Development and Racial Domination, University of the Western Cape, 8–10 October 1984.

7. Nigel Worden, *Slavery in Dutch South Africa* (Cambridge: Cambridge University Press, 1985), p. 121.

8. The two most notable slave outbreaks occurred in the Swartland in 1808 and the Bokkeveld in 1825. See R. Ross, *Cape of Torments: Slavery and Resistance in South Africa* (London: Routledge and Kegan Paul, 1983), pp. 97–116.

9. J. Mason, 'Slaveholder Resistance to the Amelioration of Slavery at the Cape'. A paper read at a conference on 'The Western Cape: Roots and Realities', 16–17 July 1986.

10. Nigel Worden, *Cape Slave Emancipation and Rural Labour in a Com-*

parative Context (Centre for African Studies, University of Cape Town, 1983).

11. Shula Marks, 'Khoisan Resistance', p. 57.

12. Richard Elphick, *Kraal and Castle*, p. 76.

13. Marks, 'Khoisan Resistance', p. 67.

14. *Ibid.*, p. 68.

15. *Ibid.*, p. 64.

16. Henry Bredenkamp and Susie Newton-King, 'The Subjugation of the Khoisan', p. 11. Also Marks, 'Khoisan Resistance', p. 68.

17. Bredenkamp and Newton-King, p. 11.

18. Marks, 'Khoisan Resistance', p. 75; M. W. Spilhaus, *South Africa in the Making 1652–1802* (Cape Town: Juta, 1966), pp. 271–3, 303–310.

19. Bredenkamp and Newton-King, pp. 29–31.

20. Freda Troup, *South Africa: An Historical Introduction* (London: Eyre Methuen, 1972), p. 95.

21. W. M. Macmillan, *Bantu, Boer and Briton: The Making of the South African Native Problem* (Oxford: Clarendon Press, 1963), pp. 61–62. Also T. R. H. Davenport, *South Africa: A Modern History* (London: Macmillan Press, 1977) p. 103.

22. Beinart and Bundy, *Hidden Struggles*, pp. 46–47.

23. Jeff Guy, *The Destruction of the Zulu Kingdom* (Johannesburg: Ravan Press, 1982), p. 58.

24. C. Villa-Vicencio, *Trapped in Apartheid: A Socio-Theological History of the English-Speaking Churches* (Maryknoll: Orbis. Cape Town: David Philip, 1988), especially Chapters 2 and 3.

25. Janet Hodgson, *Ntsikana's 'Great Hymn': A Xhosa Expression of Christianity in the Early 19th-Century Eastern Cape* (Cape Town: Centre for African Studies, University of Cape Town, 1981).

26. For an account of this campaign see Ben Maclennan, *A Proper Degree of Terror: John Graham and the Cape's Eastern Frontier* (Johannesburg: Ravan Press, 1986), p. 128.

27. Quoted in Edward Roux, *Time Longer than Rope: A History of the Black Man's Struggle for Freedom in South Africa* (Madison, Wisconsin: University of Wisconsin Press, 1964), p. 13.

28. *Ibid.*, p. 14.

29. J. K. Bokwe, *Ntsikana: The Story of an African Convert* (Lovedale Press, 1914).

30. J. B. Peires, *The House of Phalo: A History of the Xhosa People in the Days of Their Independence* (Johannesburg: Ravan Press, 1981), p. 73.

31. Roux, *Time*, p. 16.

32. G. M. Theal, *The History of South Africa from 1795–1872.* Quoted in Roux, *Time*, p. 35.

33. See Donovan Williams (ed.), *The Journal and Selected Writings of the Reverend Tiyo Soga* (Rhodes University, The Graham's Town Series. Cape Town: A.A. Balkema, 1986).

34. Roux, p. *Time*, 78.

35. First published in *Imvo Zabantsundu*, September 1896. Quoted in Glenda Kruss, *Religion, Class and Culture: Indigenous Churches in South Africa, with Special Reference to the Zionist Apostolic Church* (MA thesis submitted to the Department of Religious Studies, University of Cape Town, October 1985), p. 80.

36. Quoted in Beinart and Bundy, *Hidden Struggles*, p. 227.

37. *Ibid.*, p. 252.

38. *Ibid.*, p. 255.

39. See Robert Edgar, *Because They Chose the Plan of God.*

40. *Ibid.*, p. 39.

41. C. W. de Kiewiet, *The Imperial Factor in South Africa* (Cambridge: University Press, 1937), p. 159.

42. C. Villa-Vicencio, *Trapped in Apartheid*, Chapters 2 and 3.

43. James Cochrane, *Servants of Power: The Role of English-Speaking Churches 1903–1930* (Johannesburg: Ravan Press, 1987), p. 25.

44. Peter Delius, *The Land Belongs to Us* (Johannesburg: Ravan Press, 1983), p. 168.

45. Sol Plaatje, *Native Life in South Africa: Before and After the European War and Boer Rebellion* (London: P. J. King and Son, 1916). See also William Beinart, Peter Delius and Stanley Trapido (eds.), *Putting the Plough to the Ground: Accumulation and Dispossession in Rural South Africa 1850–1930* (Johannesburg: Ravan Press, 1986), p. 46.

46. Jeff Guy, *The Destruction of the Zulu Kingdom*, p. 58.

47. Roux, *Time*, p. 47.

48. Jeff Guy, *The Heretic: A Study of the Life of John William Colenso, 1814–1883* (Johannesburg: Ravan Press, 1983).

49. Beinart and Bundy, *Hidden Struggles*, pp. 191–221.

50. *Ibid.*, p. 191.

51. *Ibid.*, p. 218.

52. M. Horrell, *The Education of the Coloured People in South Africa: 1652–1970* (Johannesburg: S. A. Institute of Race Relations, 1970), p. 3.

53. *Ibid.*, p. 3. Also C. Villa-Vicencio, *Trapped in Apartheid*, p. 96.

54. Janet Hodgson, 'Zonnebloem College and Cape Town: 1858–1870', in *History of Cape Town*, ed. C. Saunders (Cape Town: UCT, 1979), pp. 1–16.

55. *Ibid.*

56. Quoted in Frank Molteno, 'The Historical Foundations of the Schooling of Black South Africans,' in Peter Kallaway (ed.), *Apartheid and Education: The Education of Black South Africans* (Johannesburg: Ravan Press, 1986), p. 67.

57. J. Cock, *Maids and Madams: A Study of the Politics of Exploitation* (Johannesburg: Ravan Press, 1980), p. 280.

58. Molteno in Kallaway, *Apartheid*, pp. 74–88.

59. C. Tilley, *As Sociology Meets History* (Orlando, Florida: Academic Press, 1981), p. 151.

60. Jonathan Hyslop, 'Food, Authority and Politics: Student Riots in South Africa 1945–1976', *Africa Perspective* (New Series 1, 3–4, June 1987), p. 6.

61. H. Bernstein, *For Their Triumphs and For Their Tears: Women in Apartheid South Africa* (London: IDAF, 1985), p. 7.

62. The phrase 'most oppressed of the oppressed' is from the document 'The Role of Women in the Struggle for Liberation in Zimbabwe, Namibia and South Africa', submitted to the World Conference of the United Nations Decade for Women, Copenhagen, July 1980. It is quoted in Hilda Bernstein, *Triumphs*, p. 81.

63. Beinart and Bundy, *Hidden Struggles*, p. 228.

64. Cherryl Walker, *Women and Resistance in South Africa* (New York: Onyx Press, 1982), p. 27.

65. Plaatje, *Native Life*, p. 94.

66. Quoted in Walker, *Women*, p. 31.

67. *Ibid.*

68. Shula Marks, *Reluctant Rebellion. The 1906–08 Disturbances in Natal* (Oxford: Clarendon Press, 1970), pp. 171–242.

2   Modern resistance

1. Eddie Webster, 'Background of the Supply and Control of Labour in the Gold Mines', in *Essays in Southern African Labour History* (Johannesburg: Ravan Press, 1983), p. 10.

2. Don Ncube, *Black Trade Unions in South Africa* (Johannesburg: Skotaville, 1985), pp. 14–15.

3. Webster, *Background*, p. 11.

4. Julius Lewin, *Politics and Law in South Africa* (London: Merlin Press, 1963), pp. 90f.

5. Thomas Pakenham, *The Boer War* (London: Weidenfeld and Nicolson, 1979), p. 45.

6. Webster, 'Background', p. 10.

7. Greg Cuthbertson, 'The English-Speaking Churches and Colonialism' in C. Villa-Vicencio (ed.), *Theology and Violence: The South African Debate* (Johannesburg: Skotaville, 1987), pp. 22–27.

8. P. Warwick, *Black People and the South African War: 1899–1902* (Johannesburg: Ravan Press, 1983), pp. 181–4.

9. C. Villa-Vicencio, *Trapped in Apartheid: A Socio-Theological History of the English-Speaking Churches*, p. 71.

10. See p. 22 of Chapter 1. Also R. Gray, 'Christianity, Colonialism and Communities in Sub-Saharan Africa', *Journal of Black Studies*, 13, 1, 1982, pp. 59–72.

11. Bernard Magubane, 'Imperialism and the Making of the South African Working Class' in Bernard Magubane and Nzongola-Ntalaja (eds.), *Proletarianization and Class Struggle in Africa* (San Francisco: Syn-

thesis Publications, 1983), p. 29.

12. Frederick Johnstone, 'A Comment', *Journal of the Fernand Braudel Center*, 3, 2 (Fall), quoted in Magubane, p. 30.

13. E. Roux, *Time*, p. 148.

14. C. W. de Kiewiet, *A History of South Africa, Social and Economic* (London: Oxford University Press, 1966), p. 172.

15. Thomas Karis and Gwendolyn Carter (eds.), *From Protest to Challenge: A Documentary History of African Politics in South Africa* (Stanford: Hoover Institution Press, 1977), 1, p. 53.

16. Fatima Meer, 'African Nationalism: Some Inhibiting Factors', in Heribert Adam (ed.), *South Africa: Sociological Perspectives* (London: Oxford University Press, 1971), p. 128.

Not until the establishment of the Congress Youth League in 1944 did the character of the ANC begin to change, and only at the time of the defiance campaign in the 1950s did it become a mass-based organisation.

17. For discussion on 'coloured' politics see Richard van der Ross, 'The Founding of the African People's Organisation in Cape Town in 1903 and the Role of Dr Abdurahman', *Munger Africana Library Notes*, 28, February 1975.

In later years the 'coloured' constituency, committed to a non-racial and democratic South Africa, divided along ideological lines. It was a division between those committed to the inclusive programme of resistance of the ANC and those influenced by a theoretically 'purer' classist notion of liberation. The former saw the latter as living in a 'never-never land of dialectic theory'. The latter, in turn, saw the pragmatism of the former as tantamount to 'collaboration'. They dismissed the ANC programme of action leading to the defiance campaign as 'unprincipled' displays of 'unedifying childishness'. They formed the Non-European Unity Movement (NEUM) in 1943. The more recent New Unity Movement stands within the tradition of the NEUM.

18. Cherryl Walker, *Women and Resistance in South Africa* (New York: Onyx Press, 1982), p. 36.

Despite a lull in organised national work, women remained active through local church and community groups, but also through the Communist Party of South Africa's involvement in trade unionism. In 1933 the National Council of African Women was formed, and in 1954 the Federation of South African Women (FEDSAW)

19. A. Lerumbo, *Fifty Fighting Years: The South African Communist Party, 1921–1971* (London: Inkululeko Publications, 1971). Quoted in Magubane, p. 38.

20. See Ncube, pp. 29–48. Also, Philip Bonner, 'The Decline and Fall of the ICU: A Case of Self-Destruction?' in Webster (ed.), *Essays in Southern African Labour History* (Johannesburg: Ravan Press, 1983), pp. 114–120.

21. The CPSA was disbanded shortly before the Suppression of Communism Act was enacted into law in 1950, and reconstituted underground

as the South African Communist Party in 1953.

22. Surendra Bhana and Bridglal Pachai (eds.), *A Documentary History of Indian South Africans* (Cape Town: David Philip, 1984), p. 150.

In 1947, under Drs. G. M. Naicker and Y. M. Dadoo, the SAIC formed a pact with the ANC under the leadership of Dr. A. B. Xuma. Conservative Indians would twenty years later (in 1968) introduce an alternative thrust in Indian politics by agreeing to serve on the South African Indian Council, as part of the apartheid structure of government.

23. See also J. W. de Gruchy, *Cry Justice* (London: Collins, 1986), p. 63.

24. Quoted in James Cochrane, *Servants of Power: The Role of English-Speaking Churches 1903–1930* (Johannesburg: Ravan Press, 1987), p. 113.

25. C. Villa-Vicencio, *Trapped in Apartheid*, pp. 53f.

26. *Ibid.*, p. 157.

27. The report of a Commission of Inquiry into the strikes, quoted in Webster, 'Background', p. 5.

28. See p. 41 of this chapter.

29. Tom Lodge, *Black Politics in South Africa Since 1945* (Johannesburg: Ravan Press, 1983), p. 7.

30. W. A. de Klerk, *The Puritans in Africa* (London, Collins, 1976), p. 104.

31. Karis and Carter, *From Protest*, 2, p. 60.

32. *Ibid.*, p. 308.

33. Magubane, 'Imperialism', p. 43.

34. *Ibid.*, p. 41.

35. Ncube, pp. 90f.

36. Karis and Carter, *From Protest*, 2, pp. 458–65.

37. *Ibid.*, 2, pp. 486–488.

38. See B. Rose and R. Tunmer, *Documents in South African Education* (Johannesburg: Ad Donker, 1975), pp. 260–67.

39. Trevor Huddleston, *Naught for Your Comfort* (London: Collins, 1956), p. 171.

40. Quoted in Alan Paton, *Apartheid and the Archbishop: The Life and Times of Geoffrey Clayton* (New York: Charles Scribner's, 1973), p. 240.

41. See Raymond Suttner and Jeremy Cronin, *Thirty Years of the Freedom Charter* (Johannesburg: Ravan Press, 1985).

42. Lodge, *Black Politics*, pp. 141–145.

43. Gail Gerhart, *Black Power in South Africa: The Evolution of an Ideology* (Berkeley: University of California Press, 1978), pp. 173–211.

44. Lodge, *Black Politics*, p. 223.

45. *Ibid.*

46. See J. de Gruchy and C. Villa-Vicencio (ed.), *Apartheid is a Heresy* (Cape Town: David Philip. Grand Rapids: Eerdmans, 1983).

47. Karis and Carter, *From Protest*, 3, p. 772.

48. *Ibid.*, p. 717.

49. Gerhart, *Black Power*, p. 14.

50. Tom Lodge, 'The Poqo Insurrection', in Tom Lodge (ed.) *Resistance and Ideology in Settler Societies* (Johannesburg: Ravan Press, 1986), p. 183.

5. Quoted in *ibid.*, p. 185.

52. Karis and Carter, *From Protest*, 3, p. 772.

53. *Trapped in Apartheid*, pp. 109–117.

54. Gerhart, *Black Power*, p. 274.

55. *Ibid.*, p. 262.

56. *Ibid.*, p. 265.

57. *Ibid.*, p. 285.

58. Jeremy Keenan, 'Reform and Resistance in the South African Bantustans, in *South African Review*, 4 (Johannesburg: Ravan Press, 1987), pp. 117–136.

59. See, for example, Allan Boesak, *Farewell to Innocence* (Maryknoll: Orbis Books, 1977).

60. Philip Bonner, 'Overview: Strikes and the Independent Trade Unions', in Johan Maree (ed.), *The Independent Trade Unions: 1974–1984* (Johannesburg: Ravan Press, 1987), p. 58.

61. John Kane-Berman, *Soweto: Black Revolt, White Reaction* (Johannesburg: Ravan Press, 1978), pp. 1–10.

62. For a detailed history of the Christian Institute see P. Walshe, *Church Versus State in South Africa: The Case of the Christian Institute* (Maryknoll: Orbis Books, 1983).

63. Tom Lodge, 'Mayihlome! Let us go to war!: From Nkomati to Kabwe, The ANC, January 1984–June 1985,' *South African Review 3* (Johannesburg: Ravan Press, 1986), p. 226.

64. Speech delivered at the launch of the UDF at Mitchells Plain, Cape Town, 20 August 1983.

65. *Trapped in Apartheid*, pp. 153–168.

66. Published by Orbis Books in the United States and David Philip in South Africa in 1988.

67. *Trapped in Apartheid*, pp. 115–117.

3   Civil disobedience

1. Martin Luther King, *Why We Can't Wait* (New York: New American Library, 1963), pp. 76–95.

2. Alexander M. Bickel, *The Morality of Consent* (New Haven and London: Yale University Press, 1975), pp. 93, 122, 95.

3. Gerald Gordon QC, 'World Courts do not absolve those who are ordered to kill,' *Cape Times*, 16 October 1987.

4. *Cape Times*, 16 October 1987.

5. H. W. van der Merwe, 'A Plea for Conscientious Affirmation', *The Friend*, 145, 4, 3 April 1987, pp. 415–416.

6. André du Toit, 'Civil Obedience and Disobedience', *Pro Veritate*, 12, July 1973, pp. 15–19.

7. Hannah Arendt, 'Civil Disobedience', in Eugene Rostow (ed), *Is Law Dead?* (New York: Simon and Schuster, 1971), pp. 219–20.

8. 'The Epistle Concerning the Martyrdom of Polycarp', in Alexander Roberts and James Donaldson (eds), *The Ante-Nicene Fathers*, 1: *The Apostolic Fathers with Justin Martyr and Irenaeus* (Grand Rapids: Eerdmans, n.d.), pp. 31–36.

9. John Calvin, *Institutes of the Christian Religion*, edited by John T. McNeill (Philadelphia: Westminster Press, 1960), IV, xx, 3,32.

10. Michael Walzer, *The Revolution of the Saints* (Cambridge, Mass.: Harvard University Press, 1965), p. 65.

11. *Praelections on Jeremiah*, quoted in Robert H. Murray, *The Political Consequences of the Reformation* (New York: Russell and Russell, 1960), p. 99.

12. Karl Barth, *Church Dogmatics* (Edinburgh: T. and T. Clark, 1957), II/I, p. 386; *Epistle to the Romans* (London: Oxford University Press, 1960), p. 493.

13. Allan Boesak, *Black and Reformed: Apartheid, Liberation and the Calvinist Tradition* (Maryknoll: Orbis, 1984). See also, John de Gruchy, 'The Revitalization of Calvinism in South Africa: Some Reflections on Christian Belief, Theology, and Social Transformation', *Journal of Religious Ethics*, 14, 1, Spring 1986, pp. 22–47.

14. Karl Barth, *Church Dogmatics* (Edinburgh: T. and T. Clark, 1957), II/I, p. 444.

15. Dietrich Bonhoeffer, *No Rusty Swords: Letters, Lectures and Notes, 1928–1936* (New York: Harper and Row, 1965), p. 225. Karl Barth, *Church Dogmatics* (Edinburgh: T. and T. Clark, 1957), II/I, p. 444.

16. C. Villa-Vicencio, 'Archbishop Desmond Tutu: From Oslo to Cape Town', in Buti Tlhagale and Itumeleng Mosala (eds), *Hammering Swords into Ploughshares* (Grand Rapids: Eerdmans. Trenton: Africa World Press, 1986), pp. 1–11.

17. Paul Tillich, 'What is Wrong with Dialectical Theology?' *Journal of Religion*, 15 (1935), p. 135. See also, John M. Mulder, 'Calvinism, Politics and the Ironies of History', *Religion in Life*, 47, Summer 1978.

18. King, *Why We Can't Wait*, 82.

19. Quoted from a sermon preached at St George's Cathedral, Cape Town on 13 March 1988 at a church service called in protest against restrictions placed on seventeen democratic organisations.

20. John Rawls, *A Theory of Justice* (Cambridge: Harvard University Press, 1971).

21. Robert Bellah, *Beyond Belief* (New York: Harper and Row, 1970), p. 130.

22. Michael Walzer, 'The Obligation to Disobey the Law', in D. Don Welch (ed), *Law and Morality* (Philadelphia: Fortress Press, 1987), p. 143.

23. John Locke, *The Second Treatise of Government* in *Two Treatises of Civil Government* (London: J. M. Dent and Sons. New York: E. P. Dutton, 1949), paras. 199–224.

24. Quoted in Walzer, 'Obligation', p. 129.

25. Locke, *Treatise*, paras.199–224.

26. St Augustine, *The City of God*, XIX, 24, in Schaff (ed.), *Nicene and Post Nicene Fathers* 1st. series, 2 (Grand Rapids, Eerdmans, n.d.). See also Villa-Vicencio, 'Tutu', pp. 20–38.

27. St Thomas Aquinas, *Summa Theologica* (London: Blackfriars, 1964), 1a2ae (93.3); 2a2ae (42.2); 2a2ae (104.6).

28. Martin Luther, 'Secular Authority: To What Extent Should It Be Obeyed?' in *Works of Luther*, 45 (Philadelphia: Muhlenberg Press, 1959), pp. 75–129.

29. Quoted in Roland Bainton, *Here I Stand* (Nashville: Abingdon, 1950), p. 231.

30. Martin Luther, 'Interpretation of Psalm 101', quoted in H. G. Haile, *Luther: An Experiment in Biography* (Princeton: Princeton University Press, 1980), p. 101.

31. See, *inter alia*, 'Treatise of Good Works', in *Works of Luther* (Philadelphia: Muhlenberg Press, 1959), 44, p. 95; 'To the Christian Nobility,' *LW*, 44, pp. 212–15; 'To the Nobles of Germany,' *LW*, 45, pp. 355–78. For a more positive reading of Luther's political theology see Ulrich Duchrow, *Christenheit und Weltverantwortung: Traditionsgeschichte und Systematische Struktur der Zweireichelehre* (Stuttgart: Klett-Cotla, 1983).

32. Jürgen Moltmann, *On Human Dignity: Political Theology and Ethics* (London: SCM, 1984), p. 70.

33. C. Villa-Vicencio, 'Theology in the Service of the State', in C. Villa-Vicencio and J. W. de Gruchy (eds), *Resistance and Hope: Essays in Honour of Beyers Naudé* (Cape Town: David Philip. Grand Rapids: Eerdmans, 1986), pp. 112–125.

34. Quoted in John Coleman, 'Reinhold Niebuhr's Political Theology', *The Ecumenist*, 24, 6, September–October 1986, p. 87.

35. Rubem Alves, *Tomorrow's Child: Imagination, Creativity and the Rebirth of Culture* (London: SCM Press, 1972), p. 111.

36. Bickel, *Morality*, pp. 3–4.

37. Lord Patrick Devlin, 'Moral and Criminal Law', in D. D. Welch (ed.), *Law and Morality* (Philadelphia: Fortress Press, 1987), p. 18.

38. See pp. 106ff.

39. John Austin, *The Province of Jurisprudence Determined* (Library of Ideas ed., 1954), p. 184.

40. Hans Kelsen, *General Theory of Law and State* (Cambridge, Mass.: Harvard University Press, 1945), p. 113.

41. H. L. A. Hart, 'Positivism and the Separation of Law and Morals', *Harvard Law Review*, 71, 1957–58, p. 603.

42. *Ibid.*, p. 617.

43. Bickel, *Morality*, p. 17.

44. See also pp. 107ff.

45. Lon Fuller, 'Positivism and Fidelity to Law – A Reply to Professor

Hart', *Harvard Law Review*, 72, 1957–58, pp. 642–643.

46. For further discussion see Chapter 6, pp. 132ff.

47. Karl Marx, 'German Ideology', in David McLellan (ed.), *Selected Works* (Oxford: Oxford University Press, 1977), p. 76.

48. Bickel, *Morality*, p. 12.

49. Devlin, in Welch (ed.), *Law*, p. 41.

50. Bickel, *Morality*, p. 17.

5. A statement of the Convocation issued as part of a press release by the General Secretary of the SACC, on 2 June 1988.

52. Bickel, *Morality*, p. 17

53. Walter Wink, *Jesus' Third Way: Violence and Nonviolence in South Africa*, p. 4.

54. In Villa-Vicencio, *Between Christ and Caesar*, p. 249.

55. *The Kairos Document: Challenge to the Churches*, second revised edition (Johannesburg: Skotaville, 1986), p. 22.

56. Barnard Häring, *The Law of Christ: Moral Theology for Priests and Laity*, 3 (Cork: Mercier Press, 1967), p. 150. Quoted in A. Nolan, 'The Day of Prayer and Catholic Moral Theology', in A. Boesak and C. Villa-Vicencio (eds), *When Prayer Makes News* (Philadelphia: Westminster Press, 1986), p. 94.

57. A. Nolan, *ibid.*, p. 95.

58. Statement of the Convocation of Churches, which met in Johannesburg 30–31 May 1988.

59. Aquinas, *Summa Theologica*, 2a2ae (42,2).

4 War, tyranny and revolution

1. *The Kairos Document: Challenge to the Churches*, p. 13.

2. Quoted in Alexander Bickel, *The Morality of Consent* (New Haven and London: Yale University Press, 1975), p. 44.

3. See also Chapters 1 and 2.

4. T. Karis and G. Carter (eds), *From Protest to Challenge*, 3 (Stanford: Hoover Institution Publications, 1977), p. 740.

5. For a consideration of the history of the church's response to the problem of violence see C. Villa-Vicencio (ed.), *Theology and Violence: The South African Debate* (Johannesburg: Skotaville, 1987).

6. For a fuller discussion on just war theory see the articles in *Theology and Violence* by Douglas Bax, 'From Constantine to Calvin: The Doctrine of the Just War', as well as Albert Nolan and Mary Armour, 'Armed Struggle as a Last Resort: The Roman Catholic Position'.

7. St Augustine, *The City of God*, XV, 4 (Garden City: Image Books, 1958).

8. St Augustine, *Quaestiones et Locutiones in Heptateuchum*, VI, X. Quoted in W. O'Brien, *The Conduct of Just and Limited War* (New York: Praeger, 1981), p. 20.

9. Martin Luther, 'Whether Soldiers, Too, Can Be Saved', in *Luther's*

Works, edited by R. C. Schultz (Philadelphia: Fortress Press, 1967), 46, pp. 118–222.

10. John Calvin, *Institutes of the Christian Religion*, edited by John T. McNeill (Philadelphia: Westminster Press, 1960), IV, xx.12.

11. James Childress, 'Just War Criteria' in T. A. Shannon (ed.), *War or Peace* (Maryknoll: Orbis, 1980), p. 40.

12. See John H. Yoder, *Karl Barth and the Problem of War* (Nashville: Abingdon Press, 1970), p. 41.

13. Philip J. Murion (ed.), *Catholics and Nuclear War: A Commentary on the Challenge of Peace* (London: Geoffrey Chapman, 1983), p. 169.

14. *Cape Times*, 23 March 1987.

15. Martin Luther, 'Secular Authority: To What Extent It Should Be Obeyed?' in *Luther's Works* (Philadelphia: Muhlenberg Press, 1959), 45.

16. Thomas Aquinas, *Summa Theologica* (London: Blackfriars, 1964), 2a2ae.42,2.

17. Thomas Aquinas, *On Kingship*, X, 80–81, in Dino Bigongiari (ed.), *The Political Ideas of St Thomas Aquinas* (New York: Hafner, 1969).

18. Luther, 'Secular Authority: To What Extent It Should Be Obeyed?'

19 John Calvin, *Institutes of the Christian Religion*, edited by J. T. McNeill, IV, xx.12.

20. Theodore Beza, *Concerning the Rights of Rulers over Their Subjects and the Duty of Subjects Towards Their Rulers* (Cape Town: HAUM, 1956). Also J. G. Davies, *Christians, Politics and Violent Revolution* (Maryknoll: Orbis, 1976.) pp. 50f.

21. See C. Villa-Vicencio, *Between Christ and Caesar: Classic and Contemporary Texts on Church and State* (Cape Town: David Philip. Grand Rapids: Eerdmans, 1986), pp. 60–85.

22. Pope Paul VI, *Populorum Progressio*, in M. Walsh and B. Davies (eds), *Proclaiming Justice and Peace* (London: Collins, 1984), p. 141.

23. Donal Dorr, *Option for the Poor: A Hundred Years of Vatican Social Teaching* (Maryknoll: Orbis, 1983), p. 161.

24. Society for the Propagation of the Faith, *Instruction on Christian Freedom and Liberation* (Vatican City, 1986), pp. 46–47.

25. Kenneth Kaunda, *Kaunda on Violence*, edited by Colin M. Morris (London: Collins, 1980), p. 107.

26. For a discussion on the attitude of the WCC to the South African liberation movements' resort to violence see my 'Ecumenical Debate: Violent Revolution and Military Disarmament', in *Theology and Violence*.

27. Published in *The Churches' Search for Justice and Peace in Southern Africa: Report on Meeting in Lusaka, Zambia, 4–8 May 1987* (Geneva: WCC, 1987), pp. 28–9.

28. Desmond Tutu, 'Freedom Fighters or Terrorists?' in C. Villa-Vicencio (ed.), *Theology and Violence*, pp. 76–77.

29. Joseph Lelyveld, *Move Your Shadow: South Africa, Black and White* (Johannesburg: Jonathan Ball. London: Michael Joseph, 1986), p. 328.

30. K. Barth, *Church Dogmatics* III/4 (Edinburgh: T. & T. Clark, 1961), p. 453; *The Knowledge of God and the Service of God According to the Teaching of the Reformation* (London: Hodder and Stoughton, 1938), p. 231. See also John Howard Yoder, *Karl Barth and the Problem of War* (Nashville: Abingdon Press, 1970), for a critique of Barth's *Grenzfall* ethic.

31. *Weekly Mail,* 15 February 1985.

32. *The Argus,* 25 April 1987.

33. Desmond Tutu, 'Freedom Fighters or Terrorists?' in C. Villa-Vicencio (ed.), *Theology and Violence,* p. 77.

34. Frank Chikane, 'Where the Debate Ends', in C.Villa-Vicencio (ed.), *Theology and Violence,* p. 304.

35. Paul Lehmann, *The Transfiguration of Politics* (New York: Harper and Row, 1975), especially pp. 259–275.

36. *Instruction on Christian Freedom and Liberation,* p. 46.

5   State illegitimacy

1. *The Kairos Document: A Theological Comment on the Political Crisis in South Africa,* revised second edition (Johannesburg: Skotaville, 1986), p. 22.

2. See *The Churches' Search for Justice and Peace in Southern Africa: Report on Meeting in Lusaka, Zambia, 4–8 May 1987* (Geneva: WCC, 1987), p. 28.

3. C. Villa-Vicencio, *Trapped in Apartheid,* pp. 165f.

4. Frank Chikane, 'Where the Debate Ends', in C.Villa- Vicencio (ed.), *Theology and Violence,* p. 308.

5. Gregory Baum, 'Peter Berger's Unfinished Symphony', in Gregory Baum (ed.), *Sociology and Human Destiny* (New York: Seabury, 1980), p. 119.

6. H. L. A. Hart, 'Positivism and the Separation of Law and Morals', *Harvard Law Review,* 7, 1957–58, p. 594.

7. *Ibid.,* pp. 615–621.

8. *Ibid.,* p. 603.

9. *Ibid.,* p. 617.

10. Lon L. Fuller, 'Positivism and the Fidelity to Law – A   Reply to Professor Hart', *Harvard Law Review,* 71, 1957–58, p. 656.

11. *Kairos Document,* p. 5.

12. Hart, 'Positivism', p. 617.

13. J. Rawls, *A Theory of Justice* (Oxford: Clarendon Press, 1972), p. 183.

14. Fuller, 'Positivism', pp. 642–43.

15. *Ibid.,* p. 643.

16. John Dugard, *Human Rights and the South African Legal Order* (Princeton: Princeton University Press, 1978), p. 397–8.

17. Ronald Dworkin, *Taking Rights Seriously* (Cambridge, Mass.: Harvard University Press, 1977), p. 22.

18. Ronald Dworkin, *Law's Empire* (Cambridge, Mass.: Harvard University Press, 1986), pp. 225–275.

19. *Ibid.,* p. 224.

20. Peter Gabel, in *Harvard Law Review*, 1977, 91, pp. 302–315.

21. See *inter alia* Raymond Wacks, 'Judges and Injustice', *South African Journal of Law* (hereafter *SALJ*), 101, pp. 266f; John Dugard, 'Should Judges Resign? A Reply to Professor Wacks', *SALJ*, 101, pp. 286f; *Lawyers for Human Rights Bulletin*, 3, 1984.

22. *Kairos Document*, p. 1.

23. See pp. 56ff above.

24. Ulrich Duchrow, *Global Economy: A Confessional Issue for the Churches?* (Geneva: WCC Publications, 1987), p. 86.

25. The statement is included in J. de Gruchy and C. Villa-Vicencio (eds), *Apartheid is a Heresy*, pp. 168–173.

26. *Ibid.*, pp. 160–161.

27. *Ibid.*, pp. 179–181.

28. Andrew Bradstock, *Saints and Sandinistas: The Catholic Church in Nicaragua and its Response to the Revolution* (London: Epworth Press, 1987), p. 19.

29. J. W. C. Wand, *The Four Great Heresies* (London: SCM, 1955), pp. 377f. For an application of this definition of heresy to apartheid see John W. de Gruchy, 'Towards a Confessing Church: The Implications of Heresy', in John W. de Gruchy and Charles Villa-Vicencio (eds.), *Apartheid is a Heresy*, pp. 83–86.

30. Albert Nolan, 'The Day of Prayer and Catholic Moral Theology', in *When Prayer Makes News*, p. 95.

31. For the debate on the legal status of Rhodesia after the Unilateral Declaration of Independence, see Donald B. Molteno, 'The Rhodesian Crisis and the Courts', in *The Comparative and International Law Journal of Southern Africa*, 2, 2, July 1969, pp. 254–289; 2, 3, November 1969, pp. 404–443; 3, 1, March 1970, pp. 18–49. Also *Acta Juridica 1973* (Cape Town: Juta and Company, 1975), pp. 1–171; *Acta Juridica 1974* (Cape Town: Juta and Company, 1976), pp. 109–246.

32. Molteno in *CILSA*, 2, 2, July 1968, p. 256. For a discussion on Hans Kelsen's understanding of revolution as a means of replacing an existing fundamental law (*Grundnorm*) with another see 'The Pure Theory of Law' in *Law Quarterly Review*, 51, pp. 517f.

33. Molteno, *ibid.*, pp. 256–57.

34. Molteno in *CILSA*, 2, 3, November 1969, pp. 425f.

35. J. Habermas, *Legitimation Crisis* (London: Heinemann, 1976), p. 53.

6 The church between the times

1. The notion of 'living between the times', as borrowed from Karl Barth is discussed on p. 8.

2. Anthony Sampson, *Black and Gold: Tycoons, Revolutionaries and Apartheid* (New York: Pantheon Books, 1987), p. 233. Italics are added.

3. Rubem Alves, *Tomorrow's Child: Imagination, Creativity and the Rebirth*

of Culture, pp. 1f.

4. See, *inter alia*, Julian Freund, *The Sociology of Max Weber* (London: Allen Lane, 1968).

5. Charles Villa-Vicencio, *Trapped in Apartheid*, p. 186.

6. Steve Biko, *I Write What I Like* (London: Heinemann, 1978), p. 29.

7. Quoted in Shirley du Bouley, *Tutu: Voice of the Voiceless* (London: Hodder and Stoughton, 1988), p. 44.

8. Jon Sobrino, *The True Church and the Poor* (London: SCM, 1984), p. 121.

9. See Chapter 2.

10. Compare Lawrence Schlemmer, 'South Africa's National Party Government' and Helen Zille, 'The Right Wing in South African Politics', in Peter L. Berger and Bobby Godsell (eds.), *A Future South Africa: Visions, Strategies and Realities* (Cape Town: Human and Rousseau, 1988), pp. 36–37 and pp. 80–82.

11. Annette Seegers, 'Civil-Military Relations in South Africa: A Focus on State Power', in Simon Baynham (ed.), *The South African Security Establishment* (London: Routledge and Kegan Paul, 1988). Publication awaited.

12. *Pro Mundi Vita Bulletin: The Churches of Latin America in Confrontation with the State and the Ideology of National Security*, 71, March–April 1978, p. 10.

13. *Ibid.* For a popularised statement see *Crisis News, A Bulletin of News and Theological Reflection on the South African Emergency*, 24, August 1988. Published by the Western Province Council of Churches.

14. Jose Comblin, *The Church and the National Security State* (Maryknoll: Orbis Books, 1979), p. 72.

15. *Pro Mundi Vita Bulletin*, p. 7.

16. *Ibid.*, p. 10.

17. Anne Bernstein and Bobby Godsell, 'The Incrementalists', in Peter Berger and Bobby Godsell, *Future South Africa*, pp. 70–71. See also footnote on p. 306.

18. Renfrew Christie, 'Reparations and the Economics of Moving Beyond Apartheid. A Review Essay of Peter L. Berger and Bobby Godsell (eds.), *A Future South Africa: Visions, Strategies and Realities*', in *Social Dynamics*, 14, 2, December, pp. 75–82.

19. See David Pallister, Sarah Stewart and Ian Lepper, *South Africa Inc.: The Oppenheimer Empire* (London: Simon and Schuster, 1987), p. 205.

20. *Weekly Guardian*, 24 July 1988.

21. *Congressional Record – House*, 11 August 1988.

22. Commonwealth Committee of Foreign Ministers on Southern Africa, 'South Africa's Relationship with the International Financial System. Report of the Inter-Governmental Group' (Commonwealth Secretariat, Marlborough House, London, July 1988).

23. John Kane-Berman, 'The Sanction Impact', *South African Review 4*,

July 1988.

24. Christiaan van Wyk, 'Facing the Nineties: Business Amidst Sanctions and Disinvestment', *South African Review 4*, July 1988.

25. Reported in the *Cape Times,* 30 August 1988.

26. Simon Barber, 'Washington's Best Reasons for Sanctions Against SA', in *Cape Times,* 30 August 1988.

27. Renfrew Christie, 'Reparations and the Economics of Moving Beyond Apartheid. A Review Essay of Peter L. Berger and Bobby Godsell (eds.), *A Future South Africa: Visions, Strategies and Realities*', in *Social Dynamics,* 14, 2, December, pp. 75–82.

28. Laurie Nathan, 'Resistance to Militarisation: Three Years of the End Conscription Campaign', in *South African Review 4*, p. 109.

29. *Ibid.,* p. 114.

30. Alistair Kee, *Constantine Versus Christ* (London: SCM, 1982), p. 154.

31. See Charles Villa-Vicencio, *Trapped in Apartheid,* Chapter 2.

32. See P. Lehmann, 'Karl Barth, Theologian of Permanent Revolution', *Union Seminary Quarterly Review,* 28, 1972.

33. James Cochrane, 'Christian Resistance to Apartheid: Periodisation, Prognosis', in a manuscript edited by Martin Prozesky, to be published by Macmillan Press.

34. See, for example, *Report of the Commission of Inquiry into the Mass Media* (Pretoria: Government Printer, RP 89/1981), which includes over 400 pages on the role of the churches in the South African context.

35. See discussion in Villa-Vicencio, *Trapped in Apartheid,* pp. 145–150.

36. See C. Villa-Vicencio, 'No Change in the White NGK', *Reformed Journal,* April 1989.

37. *Report of the Commission of Inquiry into the South African Council of Churches* (Pretoria: Government Printer, RP 89/1981).

38. Charles Villa-Vicencio, 'Theology in the Service of the State: the Steyn and Eloff Commissions', in Charles Villa-Vicencio and John de Gruchy (eds), *Resistance and Hope: South African Essays in Honour of Beyers Naudé,* pp. 112–125.

39. J. A. Loubser, *The Apartheid Bible: A Critical Review of Racial Theology in South Africa* (Cape Town: Maskew Miller Longman, 1987).

40. *Minutes of the One Hundred and Fourth Annual Conference of the Methodist Church of Southern Africa,* 1986, pp. 85–86.

41. *Minutes of the One Hundred and Fourth Annual Conference of the Methodist Church of Southern Africa,* 1986, pp. 340–341.

42. Walter Wink, *Jesus' Third Way* (Philadelphia: New Society Publishers, 1987).

43. Karl Barth, *Epistle to the Romans,* trans. E. C. Hoskyns (London: Oxford University Press, 1960), pp. 475–502.

44. H. Gollwitzer, 'Kingdom of God and Socialism in the Theology of Karl Barth', in G. Hunsinger (ed.), *Karl Barth and Radical Politics* (Philadelphia: Westminster Press, 1976), p. 106.

45. *Ibid.*, p. 430.

46. Karl Barth, *The Word of God and the Word of Man* (New York: Harper and Row, 1957), p. 299.

47. Paul Lehmann, *The Transfiguration of Politics* (New York: Harper and Row, 1975), p. xiii.

48. M. Horkheimer, 'Die Sehnsucht nach dem ganz Anderen: ein Interview mit kommentaar von Helmut Gumnior' (Hamburg: Furche, 1975), p. 60.

49. *The Kairos Document: Challenge to the Church*, p. 1.

50. Karl Barth, *Church Dogmatics* IV/2 (Edinburgh: T. and T. Clark, 1958), p. 180.

51. Richard Fox, *Reinhold Niebuhr: A Biography* (San Francisco: Harper and Row, 1987), p. 265.

52. Reinhold Niebuhr, 'Perils of American Power', *Atlantic Monthly*, 149, January 1932, p. 90. See Ronald H. Stone, *Reinhold Niebuhr: Prophet to Politicians* (Nashville: Abingdon Press, 1972), p. 86.

53. Reinhold Niebuhr, 'History (God) Has Overtaken Us', *Radical Religion*, VI, Summer 1941.

54. Fox, *Niebuhr*, p. 265. Karl Barth, *Against the Stream* (London: SCM, 1954), p. 107.

55. Paul Tillich, 'Reinhold Niebuhr's Doctrine of Knowledge', in Kegley and Bretall (eds), *Reinhold Niebuhr: His Religious, Social and Political Thought* (New York: Macmillan, 1956), p. 36.

56. John Coleman, 'Reinhold Niebuhr's Political Theology', in *The Ecumenist*, 24, 6, September–October 1986, p. 85, makes this point specifically with regard to *The Structure of Nations and Empires*.

57. Beverley Wildung Harrison, *Making the Connections: Essays in Feminist Social Ethics*, edited by Carol Robb (Boston: Beacon Press, 1985), pp. 22–40.

58. Alves, p. 66.

59. Dietrich Bonhoeffer, *Letters and Papers from Prison* (London: Fontana Books, 1964), p. 135.

60. Karl Rahner, *The Shape of the Church to Come* (London: SPCK, 1974), p. 79.

61. I. Bria (ed.), *Martyria/Mission* (Geneva: WCC, 1980), p. 9.

62. Wallace Stevens, *Opus Posthumus*. Quoted in Robert Bellah, 'Transcendence in Contemporary Piety', in *Beyond Belief* (New York: Harper and Row, 1970), p. 210.

63. An important discussion on the crisis of confidence in the moral tradition of political debate is found in André du Toit's inaugural lecture 'Truth and Justice in South Africa' delivered at the University of Cape Town on 14 September 1988.

64. Lehmann, *The Transfiguration of Politics*, p. 25. Also pp. 27–33.

Index